HOPE, HURDLES & HEART

Copyright © 2023

All rights reserved. No part of this publication may be reproduced, distributed, or transmitted in any form or by any means, including photocopying, recording, or other electronic or mechanical methods, without the prior written permission of the publisher, except in the case of brief quotations embodied in critical reviews and certain other noncommercial uses permitted by copyright law.

CONTENTS

INTRODUCTION 4

CHAPTER 1.
Awaken Your Inner Awesome 9

CHAPTER 2.
Break Free from Mental Barriers 15

CHAPTER 3.
Cultivate a Garden of Positive Thoughts and Habits 27

CHAPTER 4.
Visionary Thinking meets Practical Action 37

CHAPTER 5.
Owning Your journey 46

CHAPTER 6.
Riding the "Habits" Wave to Success 61

CHAPTER 7.
Hurdle Hopping: Turn Obstacles into Opportunities. 71

CHAPTER 8.
Toasting Your Triumphs 80

CHAPTER 9.
Perseverance Pays: Stay the Course. 85

CHAPTER 10.
Believe in Yourself and Watch Magic Happen 93

APPENDIX 1 96

APPENDIX 2 102

APPENDIX 3 108

INTRODUCTION

I should not be writing this. Nothing about my start in life might suggest I would end up here. I grew up on a council estate in south London, England – the equivalent of the projects in the US. I knew of successful people, but they were 'over there.' Never part of my world.

I had desires, things I wanted to do, but they were impossible dreams, no more. I had no proof I could do it. No role models, nothing. Talent was always evident in me and I was book smart, but this was not particularly helpful as my discipline was below zero and *everything* in my environment was even less supportive.

We had the most awesome parents, the most impressive people I have had the opportunity to study up close. You know what they say: *"reputation is who people think you are; character is who your family knows you are."* They scored excellently on both scales, possibly even higher on the character scale because only we knew what they really had to contend with.

Sadly, everything else competed with my goals, as well as the encouragement and example our parents offered.

And in the end, everything else almost won. When I finished state-mandated education at sixteen, the writing was on the wall; I failed my final year so badly I could not have stayed at school if I wanted to.

I will not go into detail, but before the age of 5, I had a sister who died at 12 weeks old, nursed by a mother with no familial support who was also contending with a fresh scar that went from one side of her neck to the other, the result of addressing a hyperactive thyroid gland.

INTRODUCTION

Around this time, we watched as our home was engulfed in a housefire, which we just managed to escape with the help of a passing police officer. Just two key milestones in my early years.

Again, before my fifth birthday, my father suffered two major strokes at age thirty-eight. This happened just ahead of our planned return to Nigeria and those strokes stopped him from ever working again. This misfortune, in turn, consigned us to public housing from the private arrangement we previously enjoyed.

The hurdles were stacking up for my parents. With my father recovering in hospital and three children aged seven and under, it was suggested as a 4-year-old I would start school early, reduce the load on mum, and complete the reception year twice. And that's exactly what happened.

This misfortune in our family led to a strong start to my school life. Looking back, I notice a lesson here, maybe two. Firstly, there's always a gift or a blessing in really tough experiences. Secondly, these gifts often can't be seen until years later when emotions, fear or sheer overwhelm aren't clouding your perspective.

My father died 31 years later, still paralysed on the right side of his body but full of wisdom, love, encouragement, indescribable resilience, and dignity. These attrtibutes were immediately apparent to all who met him.

A real man.

I learned what a real man is from my father and it has nothing to do with where you live, your car, earnings, or almost anything else that most people think it does. It has everything to do with showing up each day, expecting the best, not complaining and resolving to do your best whether circumstances are in your favour or not.

And he was always about living for something bigger than himself. For my dad, that was his family and God. A man of few words and such deep reserves that when he spoke, his words or the sentiment of his words could easily stay with you for a lifetime.

As most parents are, mine were ambitious for me – for all of us. I was in the top stream at secondary school having, passed the 11 plus exams and only missed out on grammar school because the rules changed in London. So abject failure at age sixteen was not expected by anyone, least of all me!

I will never forget the Saturday morning my GCE results arrived. For the first time, my father let me open the letter addressed to me. It was his way of saying, 'You're moving into adulthood now. There you go, son.'

My first step into adulthood; failure across the board. I was shocked (shows you how little self-awareness I had because I hadn't done much work. I even managed to turn up for the wrong exam one day!). I was embarrassed and worried, not for the first time.

Dad could see this, so he spoke, being absolutely committed to my success. But instead of telling me what to do, he asked what I intended to do, having squandered my potential and failed so soundly.

I said two things; firstly, I would make him proud. Secondly, I'll have to start again.

Then he spoke again. "OK."

That was it. I had to start again.

So I pushed on, with my parents' blessing and amazing support from my two brothers, coupled with discouragement from everyone else who suggested I give education a miss and get a job. But I felt there was more for me.

On reflection, failing school was a singular blessing, again, only visible in hindsight. I was forced to confront myself and realised it was time to make a call. Continue on this path of underperformance or at least have a go at pursuing my dreams.

I chose the latter.

Throughout this brief book, I will expand on some of the experiences and milestones on my journey. For now, I will tell you that kid who left school with no real qualifications went on to pass his accountancy exams and became a fellow of a chartered accountancy body. Bear in mind I left school with no qualifications whatsoever in Math.

INTRODUCTION

I also gained an honours degree in Law and rose to senior management in an FTSE 100 company (these are the top 100 listed companies on the UK Stock Exchange). There, I led the way for people of colour by becoming the first black Senior Manager, Buyer, Buying Manager, and Business Unit Manager in the organisation's history.

Ultimately, I rose to become the CEO of a nationally recognised retailer, alongside operating on boards as a professionally qualified director.

More than that, I was blessed to meet the most amazing woman who became my wife and mother to our five gorgeous children, a relentless supporter who, for almost 35 years, has provided a home environment of love, acceptance and restaurant-quality food!!

Quite a journey. And still continuing.

Some years ago, I heard someone say 'the measure of a person is not where they have risen to; it is how far they have travelled and the values they have lived by on the journey'.

I want to help you travel that great distance and achieve extraordinary things, *without compromising your character*.

The aim of this book is to help you capitalise on the powerful currents of your true potential. Practical, real-world tools provided here will support you to:

- Expand your awareness
- Define your Purpose and Values
- Develop a clear, compelling vision
- Create new habits and learn how to maintain them
- Set and approach goals effectively
- Take action to achieve your dreams; and
- Stay on track

You will learn strategies for dealing with the inevitable obstacles (hurdles) and certain failures so you can turn these bumps into exhilarating waves. You will learn from the skills, attitudes, and behaviours of a diverse group of successful people who have overcome rocky times and have had the joy of celebrating personal triumphs.

At the end of each chapter, I share other resources that may be helpful if you want to 'dig deeper'. Use the book like a manual and go where you believe you will get the most benefit, first.

I have zero concern that you might not choose to read every page. I am much more concerned that every page contains something of practical value to *someone*. Anyone.

As you journey through the pages of this book, you'll find that the experiences and lessons it contains touch on universal themes – the timeless struggle against adversity, the quest for personal growth, and the enduring power of resilience. These are not just my stories or my father's; they are echoes of a shared human experience. Across cultures and through generations, we all grapple with challenges, seek to overcome them and strive to grow stronger in the process.

This book sets out to be a mirror reflecting these common aspirations and struggles, reminding us that we are all more alike in our journey than we are different.

In the end, you will be able to rise up to life's challenges and meet them head-on, delighting in your ability to enjoy the good and grow from the bad. As we embark on this journey, we will find that there are no weaknesses, no doomsday scenarios, and no failures — only opportunities to recognise where we can flourish and grow.

And with this life dynamic, you will direct all your energy toward what you want rather than away from what you fear or wish to avoid.

Ready? Let's do it!

With love,

Sam Shosanya

CHAPTER 1.
AWAKEN YOUR INNER AWESOME

"The moment one definitely commits oneself, then providence moves too... Whatever you can do, or dream you can - begin it. Boldness has genius, power and magic in it. Begin it now."
– Goethe German writer, scientist, statesman and theatre director

It was early evening in 2010, and I had just dropped my daughter off at an learning centre providing extracurricular educational support. It was in one of the most affluent areas of Auckland, New Zealand, and rather than sit in the centre while she was learning, I would often go on a walk and enjoy the solitude.

On this day, I walked up the hill instead of down it and felt prompted to look back. I peered over my shoulder at the vast expanse of premium properties, and something just told me I could own every one of them - if I lived to my potential. Bizarre!

It was such a strong feeling I was genuinely unsettled by it, but something inside truly knew there was so much in me that was untapped. Releasing that potential would make owning what I could see unremarkable.

Now, I don't own those properties (and I'm not sure I would want to), but the revelation wasn't lost on me. The point here is some people own asset portfolios that would exceed the value of those houses. The primary difference between them and you or me is living to our potential.

Property is just an example. Your potential does not have to relate to things or a career. But there is an expression of you that is so far beyond your today that you may not be able to conceive of it now.

Your mind may have started to list the reasons others are fulfilling their potential and you aren't - a head start, family money, luck, etc. All possibly true. But here's the reality:

Resourcefulness is way more important than resources.

We are magnificent! Our potential is way greater than we might imagine. To unlock your amazing potential, you must first be clear about what you want and then commit yourself to grasp it. Boldness, genius, and power spring from your clear focus and true commitment to achieving your dreams, no matter what.

Here's a quote from Pulitzer Prize-winning composer, Gian Carlo Menotti

"Hell begins on the day God grants us a clear vision of all we might have achieved....the gifts we wasted...and all we might have done but didn't do."

I can't entirely agree with the theology, but I 100% agree with the sentiment. Don't die wondering!!

Your potential also lies within your drive and ability to take action. When your mind is trained to recognise its untapped potential in every situation, you reward yourself with increased awareness, clarity, and a heightened sense of control over formerly frustrating problems.

Imagine how freeing this will be. Things that once seemed impossible look less intimidating with your new mindset. The control is yours. This potential is always at your disposal, allowing you to overcome the obstacles you confront confidently.

Put simply, you will:

- RECOGNISE the challenge,
- SEE a *new* possibility, and
- TAKE ACTION to create that desired outcome.

Not surprisingly, this is the way many successful entrepreneurs see the world. There is a popular saying among salespeople that everybody will have three separate million-dollar opportunities cross their paths in their lifetime, but few will recognise them.

Your opinions, tastes, and attitudes are all subject to change. Still, your inner spark, the true hub of your individuality, can never be reduced or diminished by anyone but *you*.

Think of this energy as pure potential. When you focus your talents, abilities, and individuality toward a specific outcome, you *can* make it happen. While fears and doubts may creep in, with a shift in focus, you will find yourself handling things with creativity, spontaneity, and resolve.

This book will help you train your mind to see past ordinary ways of looking while continually identifying, clarifying, and adjusting your goals. It will teach you to use this awareness to focus on what matters to you most.

How do we transform a moment of insight into impactful action? The answer can be found in the stories of those who have done just that. Consider Carol Moseley Braun, who grew up in a segregated neighbourhood and rose to become a U.S. Senator. Her story is a testament to realising and acting on one's potential, regardless of the starting point.

After watching Supreme Court Justice Clarence Thomas' 1991 confirmation hearings, she decided to run for office. She seized a golden opportunity from less-than-ideal circumstances. The conduct of the all-male committee disillusioned Braun. "We all thought of the Senate as this lofty place . . . where these serious men made weighty decisions," Braun told the *New York Times* during her campaign. "Instead, we saw they were just garden-variety politicians making bad speeches. We need to open up the Senate to the voices that have been excluded."

After her election, Braun further sweetened her victory by serving on the Judiciary Committee and moving on to other achievements, including being appointed U.S. ambassador to New Zealand, where we have made our home.

Braun's story shows the enormous power available when you believe in your ability to bring about what you desire most. Her example also demonstrates the influence of disillusionment or anger in achieving goals. In this case, her observations demystified a powerful illusion. She assumed the judiciary committee members were learned, wise, and uniquely qualified men—until one simple but telling experience ripped the veil from her eyes.

OK, Great story. How does this become real for me or you? Try this exercise....

The 'What If' Visualisation Technique:

- **Step 1**: Find a quiet space where you won't be disturbed and take a few deep breaths to relax.
- **Step 2**: Visualise a scenario where you are living up to your full potential. What are you doing? Who are you with? How do you feel?
- **Step 3**: Now, ask yourself 'What if' questions to expand this vision. What if you took that course? What if you applied for that job? What if you started that project?
- **Step 4**: Write down any insights or ideas that come to you during this visualisation.
- **Step 5**: Choose one 'What If' scenario and break it down into small, actionable steps you can start taking towards it.

Or you can try this approach:

Personal Potential Mapping Exercise:

- **Step 1**: Reflect on your life and identify moments when you felt most alive and fulfilled. Write these moments down.
- **Step 2**: Analyse these moments for common themes or skills you were using. Were you leading others, solving problems, creating something, or helping someone?

- **Step 3**: Create a 'Potential Map' by listing these skills and themes. Next to each, write down how you might use these in your current life or career.
- **Step 4**: Set small, achievable goals for each week to start incorporating these skills or themes into your daily life.

Follow through and trust the process. Then see what happens.

Sometimes, anger and disillusionment get in the way but they can be great motivators if you align these emotions with your creative power rather than negativity. Increased awareness can transform the energy of anger into passion, drive and focus.

I'll close with this quote from the great Nelson Mandela:

> *"There is no passion to be found playing small— in settling for a life that is less than the one you are capable of living."*
> —**Nelson Mandela, South African Statesman**

Dig deeper....

1. **Growth Mindset by Carol S. Dweck:**
   - Think of your brain like a muscle that gets stronger with use. Dweck showed that students who viewed their intelligence this way improved in math. It's like believing that you can get better at something simply by working at it.

2. **Self-Determination Theory by Deci & Ryan:**
   - Imagine being in a classroom where you feel like what you're doing really matters, and you're not just following orders. Deci and Ryan found that students in these environments do better because they feel more connected and in control of their learning.

3. **Grit by Angela Duckworth:**
   - Duckworth's study at a military academy is fascinating. She found that determination and passion, more than smarts or physical ability, predicted who would stick through the tough training. It's about not giving up on your long-term goals.

4. **Broaden-and-Build Theory by Barbara Fredrickson:**
   - Fredrickson's idea is simple yet powerful: when we feel positive, our minds open up. She found that people experiencing joy or gratitude think more creatively and build better social connections than those who don't.

5. **Flow Theory by Mihaly Csikszentmihalyi:**
   - Csikszentmihalyi says we're happiest when we're totally absorbed in what we're doing, like a painter lost in painting or a climber focused on climbing. This 'flow' state makes activities deeply satisfying.

6. **The Pygmalion Effect by Rosenthal and Jacobson:**
   - Rosenthal and Jacobson's study is like a self-fulfilling prophecy. Teachers were told some kids would bloom academically, and those kids actually did better, just because the teachers believed in them. It shows how powerful expectations can be.

CHAPTER 2.
BREAK FREE FROM MENTAL BARRIERS

Conquer Fear and Negative Thinking

"I have offended God and mankind because my work did not reach the quality it should have."
— **Leonardo da Vinci, artist, inventor, scientist, mathematician**

I was blown away when I stumbled across the truth below. It has released me from so much self-criticism and has been one of my greatest gifts in recent times.

Your brain is designed to help you survive, not to make you happy.

This scientific fact helped me realise I am not some weirdo whose default position is looking for the bad in situations, assuming the worst, staying focused on obstacles, not possibilities.

The latest theories - in simple terms, I am no expert - indicate that the amygdala is critical in perceiving risks or danger. This almond-shaped brain region, which accounts for c0.3% of brain mass, is the dominant and default position because it seeks out danger. For a soft-skinned mammal living on a planet of things that could harm it, a good safety net in the circumstances.

However, this is not a great way to design the life you were created to live. Your brain's starting point is to focus on why not.

Knowing that we have a default position, we must intentionally fight this natural negativity. Being aware is being armed to do something about it. We have no excuses.

The amygdala, a small almond-shaped structure in our brain, plays a pivotal role in processing fear and emotional responses. When we encounter something that scares us, the amygdala activates, triggering a fear response. However, this response isn't always in proportion to the actual threat, leading to excessive anxiety or fear in certain situations. Recent studies have shown that we can moderate this response through specific techniques. For instance, mindfulness practices have been observed to reduce amygdala activity, leading to lower levels of anxiety and fear.

Mindfulness involves paying full attention to the present moment without judgment. Research using functional MRI (fMRI) scans has revealed that individuals who engage in regular mindfulness meditation show a decrease in amygdala activity. Essentially, mindfulness helps by creating a mental space where we can observe fear without being overwhelmed by it, allowing for a more measured and controlled response.

Cognitive Behavioural Therapy (CBT) is another powerful technique for moderating the amygdala's fear response. CBT works by helping individuals identify and challenge irrational fears and beliefs, gradually reducing their fear response. This therapy capitalises on the brain's plasticity, its ability to change and adapt. Studies have shown that through CBT, individuals can rewire their brain's response to fear stimuli, effectively 'teaching' the amygdala to react differently. Over time, this leads to a significant decrease in anxiety and fear-based responses, showcasing the remarkable adaptability of the human brain.

As previously noted, your potential is limitless, and every situation is a grand opportunity without a predetermined outcome. Yet, how often do you put the brakes on your potential by having a limiting thought? Have you ever said to yourself, "I'll never be able to do that" or "I'm not smart enough to do that"? Or even, "It'll never happen"?

Where do these limiting statements come from? Why do we say them? Often, words like this stem from fear. Whether it is fear of failure, fear of the unknown, fear of rejection, or fear of what others may think.

We sometimes even fear success. This is massive for me, personally.

One approach you may find helpful is eliminating the phrase "I can't!" from your vocabulary. This is not easy, but instead, tell yourself, "I don't have enough information yet" or "I haven't learned how to do that yet." Then you can go get the knowledge.

You can even say, "I don't want to."

Do you see how something as simple as shifting how you speak to yourself and others can empower and open many more possibilities for you?

A more structured approach to tackling this question follows:

Transforming "I Can't" into "How Can I?":

- **Step 1**: Identify a situation where you typically say "I can't".
- **Step 2**: Ask yourself, "How can I tackle this?" Focus on finding solutions, not dwelling on the obstacle.
- **Step 3**: Break down the challenge into smaller, manageable tasks.
- **Step 4**: Seek advice or research strategies to overcome this specific challenge.
- **Step 5**: Take action on the smallest task then celebrate this small victory to build momentum.
- **Step 6**: Reflect on the process and adjust your approach as necessary for future challenges

Attach an internal siren to the word "can't" and pay attention to this warning to avoid holding yourself back.

When an uncomfortable, fearful feeling rises within, it is all too easy to begin listing endless excuses for not taking action that pushes you outside your comfort zone. We know our brain is wired incorrectly to help us achieve the extraordinary. Unsurprisingly, the Bible tells us to be 'transformed by the renewing of our minds.'

If you want to make minor improvements, change your behaviour. If you want to make quantum changes, change your paradigm (or thinking), Stephen Covey.

I want to talk fear again as it's a big topic. You can use fear to your advantage. The trick is to redirect the energy from the fear and use it for a constructive purpose.

Take the fear of public speaking, for instance. Instead of letting this phobia stop you from speaking in public, use that fear's energy to study the art of public speaking, create a great speech, and then give your address.

Too often, we live like we have no choice. Well, your not being in action is entirely your decision – nothing to do with circumstances, experiences, information, or inspiration. You can choose it.

Most performers like actors, musicians, or even athletes experience fear before they step on their stage, field, or court. But they have learned to convert that energy to help them do their best. Many performers have said they look forward to that fearful feeling or intense nervousness before they go on stage. It tells them they will give a great performance without ever taking the situation for granted, even if they have performed the same role dozens or even a hundred times!

Most fears are not life-threatening, and by using analytical skills (housed in the brain's neocortex), we can dismantle them and remain productive. Most people are unaware of when they allow fear to dictate their thoughts and actions. However, when you consciously acknowledge that the world will not end and there is no real threat against you, you can keep moving forward despite the fear or negative thoughts that may pass through your mind.

Fear + positive action = COURAGE

Start noticing what you say to yourself about ideas, projects, and opportunities. Notice your preconceived notions and assumptions about the "way things are" or how things will turn out. Ask yourself, "What am I *really* afraid of?" Also, notice where you feel that fear in your body then consciously decide to let it go.

Most people would be surprised the quote at the start of this chapter was from Leonardo da Vinci, the preeminent painter, inventor, and mathematician.

But, just like you and I, even the most accomplished people with seemingly the least reasons for self-doubt will turn their sharpest analytical skills against themselves and end up feeling inadequate, hopeless, and disillusioned.

It has nothing to do with intelligence, desire, hope, expectations, or anything else. It is just who we are – and who we become even more like, if we do nothing about it.

For instance, Claude Monet, the famous Impressionist painter, wrote that his life was "nothing but a failure." The great Austrian writer Franz Kafka (whose short stories "The Hunger Artist" and "Metamorphosis" are required reading in many English classes) worried that there would be no proof that he was ever a writer because he would die in obscurity.

Although these masters struggled with self-doubt and lack of confidence, da Vinci, Kafka, and Monet continued to create *in spite of it*. You must, too.

Do you know anyone you respect for their knowledge or skill who also makes comments showing self-doubt or lack of self-confidence? It seems almost silly when someone you admire makes those comments. Think of that next time you have a limiting thought because chances are, it is ridiculous.

Please trust the process for the upcoming exercise. I encourage you to explore what is behind your fear. This is deep work, but persisting will show all fears relate to some sort of desire. And I suspect you will discover it is a desire to do something or be something.

I'd encourage you to commit fully to the exercise, live with the discomfort that is bound to arise, and push through to new discoveries about yourself.

To control your fear or negative thoughts, try this: Write down something that you would like to accomplish this week, and then write your worries about it, including everything you are afraid might happen concerning achieving that goal.

Be extremely specific. Then put the paper away in a drawer for a week or close the file, if you prefer digital.

Now go ahead and do what you planned to do. When the week ends, retrieve your notes and review what you have written. Almost certainly, you will find that most of your fears never materialised and, if they did, were not nearly as bad as you had imagined.

This is a great reality check.

When fear arises, our thoughts immediately go toward ensuring our survival, often drowning our capacity for rational thought and even causing us to overreact. The "fight or flight" response previously described is for handling an imminent physical threat and perceived psychological threats.

If you find yourself struggling, stop and describe your feelings and body sensations, and then note the thoughts going through your mind. This can help you calm down, focus, and move forward in a way that serves you rather than undermines you.

You can also fend off limiting thoughts and beliefs by asking yourself these questions:

- What am I missing or overlooking in this situation?
- What am I blaming myself for that I have no control over?
- What am I *really* afraid of?
- What would I do if I didn't hold onto these fears?
- Who would I be if I didn't hold onto these fears?
- What's the smallest thing I am willing to do to make progress in the desired direction?

We have already said, it can be impossible to take wise actions because we are so emotionally involved in the situation. Where this is the case, one powerful technique is to list your fears, obstacles, or challenges.

Then, to detach yourself emotionally, consider what advice you'd give a friend in the same position. Depersonalising things this way will allow you to see your situation more clearly.

Try it now. Choose a longstanding issue and approach it following the steps above. See what eventuates from this inquiry.

The most absurd *assumptions* are the lifeblood of every limiting and self-sabotaging belief. If you find that fear leads you to doubt yourself, you can bet a few illogical leaps are underlying your feelings.

Some examples: perhaps you have assumed that if a relationship falls apart, you will be alone for the rest of your life. Or, if your next PowerPoint presentation is not flawless, your career will end, and your boss will fire you on the spot, leaving you on the street to live penniless and alone! Yeah, I know – I have gone there too.

Yet, when you bring these unconscious assumptions into the light of day, you can see how they overlook any other possible outcomes, except the absolute worst.

You may have heard the term "inner critic." This voice starts chattering when you feel threatened, saying negative things like, "Why bother facing up to your fears since you're going to fail anyway?" The trouble with the inner critic is that it always presumes certain failure. By listening to it, you fail to allow yourself the opportunity to succeed.

In the same way you exercise your body, you give your mind a workout to help you develop and maintain a positive outlook, opening your mind to a broader range of life experiences.

Fear, limiting beliefs, and self-sabotage—even in small quantities—are key causes that underly limiting behaviours, such as procrastination, lack of organisational skills, under-developed self-awareness, defensiveness, and denial, to name just a few.

A critical step toward feeling great about yourself and being more focused on your life's goals is acknowledging your fears and dealing with difficulties head-on.

Here are some sage words from the legendary motivational speaker Brian Tracy:

> *"The key to success is to focus our conscious mind on things we desire, not things we fear."*

Now read the extract below, sit still for a few minutes, meditate (think on) these words, and see if they resonate with you.

If the words do resonate, what will you *CHOOSE* to do differently?

Our greatest fear is not that we are inadequate,

but that we are powerful beyond measure.

It is our light, not our darkness, that frightens us.

We ask ourselves, Who am I to be brilliant,

gorgeous, handsome, talented, and fabulous?

Actually, who are you not to be?

You are a child of God.

Your playing small does not serve the world.

There is nothing enlightened about shrinking

so that other people won't feel insecure around you.

We were born to make manifest the glory of God within us.

It is not just in some; it is in everyone.

And, as we let our own light shine,

we consciously give other people permission to do the same.

As we are liberated from our fear,

our presence automatically liberates others.

Quoted by Nelson Mandela in his inaugural speech as the President of South Africa)

As a former CEO now turned executive coach, my journey has been a tapestry of challenging leadership roles and profound personal growth. This path began with a critical realisation: while I understood the theories of fear and anxiety academically, there was a chasm between this knowledge and the real-world fears I faced while steering a company. Determined to bridge this gap, I embarked on a journey that not only transformed me as a leader but also paved the way for my transition to executive coaching.

During my tenure as CEO, I committed myself to immersive learning experiences. Leadership forums, mindfulness seminars, and executive workshops weren't just events; they were opportunities to confront and understand my deep-seated apprehensions. Meditation, initially a tool for stress relief, became a daily practice, sharpening my thinking and bringing an unprecedented level of clarity to my leadership.

But the real transformation occurred when I embraced the high-stakes challenges of the business world – projects that stretched my capabilities and dragged me into uncharted territory. This was where theory met practice, where the calculated risks and strategic decisions I made reshaped not just our company's future but my personal approach to leadership.

This experiential journey profoundly impacted my transition to executive coaching. Now, I share these insights with other leaders, helping them navigate their fears and uncertainties. I coach them to embrace challenges as catalysts for growth, to see beyond the immediate risks, and to recognise the opportunities that lie in unexplored paths. My own experiences of transforming anxiety into decisive action and uncertainty into strategic innovation now serve as a blueprint for those I mentor.

As an executve coach, I bring not just theoretical knowledge but real-world insights into overcoming fears, embracing risks, and harnessing challenges for personal and professional growth. This journey has taught me that true leadership is about continuous learning, adapting, and evolving – principles that I now instil in the leaders I coach, guiding them towards their own transformative journeys.

What is your 'why' - your Purpose?

Before we do any further work on your thinking, I would encourage you to identify your Purpose, if you haven't done so already.

Do the following exercise and please do not take any shortcuts. Ask those you trust and who know you well to help unearth your Purpose. Documenting your Purpose will make this journey to fulfilment easier and more sustainable. This is your reason for being. It is both meaningful and significant.

Don't play small. Make sure it is worthy of the best version of you.

My purpose?

> *"To release potential in people that positively impacts the world today and future generations."*

So, go ahead. Establish your *'why'* by completing the Purpose exercise at appendix 1. Then once you can describe your Purpose in a single statement, complete the Values exercise.

If you have not done this before but are thorough and prepared to be vulnerable, it will be a life-changing exercise.

Enjoy 😊

Clarifying Your Values

Ultimately, your Values will help you to regulate the relationship between your *conduct* and your *calling* (or your Purpose). Approach this exercise with the same commitment as you have the Purpose clarification one.

Please do not rush this. The more considered, focused attention you give it, the better your outcome will be. You will see overlaps between the Values/ Purpose exercises.

You will find the Values exercise at Appendix 2.

OK. A brief story to close…

Once, a high-ranking executive in a well-established corporation faced his own limiting belief that was deeply ingrained in the corporate mindset: the idea that veering off the traditional path to launch his own business was a high-risk, low-reward venture. This belief could have been a career roadblock. Instead, it became the fuel for a strategic transformation.

The executive, harnessing years of experience and leadership acumen, scrutinised this limiting belief and asked, "What if this change is the key to unlocking more innovation and greater success?" He embarked on a rigorous process of market research and strategic planning, turning scepticism into an informed, strategic launch plan.

The result was not just the birth of a new venture but a demonstration of leadership in action. The new venture, borne out of this calculated, some say, courageous decision, became a testament to the power of overcoming limiting beliefs, illustrating how such a shift in mindset can lead to surprising success and innovation in less than 2 years.

This story is mine. Why not create yours?

Digging deeper

1. **"The Gifts of Imperfection" by Brené Brown:**
   - Brown's work on embracing vulnerability and imperfection has resonated widely, influencing various domains including psychology, business, and personal development.

2. **"Self-Compassion: The Proven Power of Being Kind to Yourself" by Kristin Neff:**
   - Neff's pioneering research on self-compassion has made a significant impact, particularly in therapeutic practices and personal well-being.

3. **"Breaking the Habit of Being Yourself: How to Lose Your Mind and Create a New One" by Dr. Joe Dispenza:**
   - Dr. Dispenza's integration of neuroscience and self-help offers a unique perspective on personal transformation, appealing to a broad audience.

4. **"You Are Not Your Brain: The 4-Step Solution for Changing Bad Habits, Ending Unhealthy Thinking, and**

Taking Control of Your Life" by Jeffrey M. Schwartz and Rebecca Gladding:

- This neuroscience-based approach to overcoming negative thoughts and habits has been influential, especially for those interested in brain science and psychology.

5. **"Change Your Brain, Change Your Life: The Breakthrough Program for Conquering Anxiety, Depression, Obsessiveness, Lack of Focus, Anger, and Memory Problems" by Daniel G. Amen:**

    - Dr. Amen's work, while more specialised, offers valuable insights into the neurological aspects of mental health and personal development.

6. **"Daring Greatly: How the Courage to Be Vulnerable Transforms the Way We Live, Love, Parent, and Lead" by Brené Brown:**

    - Another influential book by Brené Brown, this work delves into the power of vulnerability in personal and professional life. Brown's research and insights on vulnerability have sparked significant interest and application in various fields, including leadership and personal growth.

CHAPTER 3.
CULTIVATE A GARDEN OF POSITIVE THOUGHTS AND HABITS

Why Positive Thinking Matters

> *"Champions aren't made in gyms. Champions are made from something they have deep inside them—a desire, a dream, a vision. They have to have last-minute stamina, they have to be a little faster, they have to have the skill and the will. But the will must be stronger than the skill."*
> **—Muhammad Ali, world champion boxer & icon**

As Muhammad Ali says in the above quote, your success has less to do with talent than with belief in yourself and the will to succeed. Talent is just a part of the equation. If you desire something strongly enough, you likely already believe you have at least some ability to achieve it.

You don't need to be a virtuoso; believing in yourself feeds your will, and your will helps you remain focused on your desire. Staying focused on what we desire makes us feel our best or most alive.

Maybe friends or family said what you want is impractical and foolish. There are always going to be "nay-sayers," but you cannot let someone else's feeling of inadequacy stop you from achieving your dreams, whether it is a parent, sibling, or "good" friend trying to "keep you from getting hurt by your own mistakes."

Every successful person has been told more than once that what they wanted to do was impossible for them to achieve. If Edison – inventor of the electrical light bulb – believed his teacher, who said he was "addled" and could not learn, we might still be sitting in the dark!

Unlikely, but you get the point.

Willpower is great and can help you to begin the journey, but I am firmly convinced it is not enough to sustain you through the many challenges you will face on the journey to success and fulfilment.

Good habits, that is, discipline more than motivation, is what will sustain you. The role of good habits cannot be overstated in determining your future. Consider the following statement:

> *"People don't decide their futures. They decide their habits, and their habits decide their futures."*
> **-Gary Keller**

Ever since I read this, it has stuck with me. I am unsure if Gary Keller coined this phrase himself, but I read it in his book "The ONE Thing." So, what does he mean?

Habits are self-reinforcing. The more you do a certain thing, the more you are likely to continue. It makes no difference whether that habit is a good one or it is self-defeating in some way; once in your mind ingrained, you will go on to repeat it.

You will know this yourself when you reflect on behaviours you display despite wanting to behave differently. A personal example follows.

I have always played sports and, as a result, have been in fairly good physical shape for most of my life, not because I moderated my food intake but more due to expending energy by participating in competitive sports.

Injuries and children informed my decision to stop, but my habit of eating the way I did never changed. This caused me to gain many kilos over several years, largely unnoticed until I became very unhappy with how I looked and felt—generally bloated and uncomfortable.

I wanted to address this. I knew what was good for me and knew what I needed to do but I could not break the habit I had formed of eating much more than I needed, even though I was exercising (geddit?) all the willpower I could.

Ultimately, I decided to make small changes, firstly to when I would eat later in the day, then onto what I would eat, which were healthier choices than I had previously made.

These changes are simple but not easy. Over a couple of months, I managed to delay my first meal until early afternoon, instead increasing my intake of water or some other low-calorie drink, which I had learned would help stave off hunger. I also cultivated a new habit of exercise (which, by the way, was no more than walking).

In no time, the weight began to fall off, and while I have had difficult moments since, I have never returned to anything near the weight I previously was.

Small changes, applied consistently, ultimately formed a new, positive habit and a much more positive mindset.

The more I followed this habit, the greater the likelihood I would continue. This has become a subconscious process, a part of what I do instead of something I must exercise willpower to do.

Nowadays, if I eat any earlier than 1.30 pm, I am not as lucid in my thinking and run out of energy far earlier in the day.

Creating new habits, such as each day doing the one thing that would make all other tasks easier or unnecessary, will take you to your desired future. Willpower will not keep you on the right road for long – much less get you to the ultimate destination. Remember the following:

"A habit is the intersection of knowledge, skill, and desire." Covey

As a coach and consultant, guiding others through their professional and personal challenges, I often found myself wrestling with internal self-doubt. Despite my role in advising others, I questioned my own abilities and decisions.

This personal struggle resonated deeply with Stanford University's 2021 research on self-affirmation and its impact on decision-making and confidence.

Intrigued and inspired, I began integrating daily affirmations into my morning routine. Standing in front of the mirror each day, I would assert my strengths and reaffirm my commitment to guiding my clients with integrity and insight. These affirmations were not just optimistic statements but were rooted in my real achievements and the positive feedback I had received.

This practice brought a transformative change not only in my self-perception but also in my professional interactions. I started approaching client sessions with a renewed sense of confidence and clarity. The quality of my questions improved, as did my ability to connect with and empower my clients. They began to notice and comment on the positive changes in my approach, which further reinforced my belief in the power of this practice.

This experience became a testament to the effectiveness of incorporating research-backed methods into everyday life. It also reinforced the importance of coaches and consultants practising what they preach. By addressing my self-doubt through scientific strategies, I not only enhanced my professional performance but also deepened my understanding of the challenges my clients face, making me a more empathetic and effective coach and consultant.

What follows is the anatomy of habit creation – a scientific approach.

Neuroscience has moved on in leaps and bounds in recent years, and there are now so many avenues from which to gain new knowledge from top-tier researchers who have made it their life's work to share this information and make it accessible to as many people as possible.

A lot has been said about creating habits, and much of it is outdated or just plain misleading. The latest research suggests it takes closer to 66 days or at least a couple of months of consistent behaviour to create a new habit. And there's also an understanding that certain key components must exist for a new habit to be formed.

Good to know! Now see below for five steps that will help you create new habits.....and maintain them.

1. A **reason** – clear, strong, and compelling.

2. A **trigger** – what circumstances can you use as a trigger? Make this short and specific.

3. A **micro-habit** – make it something small and easy to do [less than 60 seconds].

4. **Effective practice** – (1) Do small chunks of the bigger action (2) Keep repeating (3) Notice when it goes well and celebrate. In other words, be mindful of your progress.

    - It is impossible to overstate the importance of celebrations, no matter how small. Each celebration will release a neurochemical called dopamine which drives rewards and motivation in the brain. Therefore, each celebration will make it more likely you will continue to push forward through any obstacles.

5. **A plan** – things will go wrong no matter how committed you are. You need a plan for getting back on track.

How does this work in real life? Another personal example.

I read somewhere every man should be able to do 30 full-body push-ups. Back in my sporting days, no problem. Having had years out of the gym and zero time doing upper body exercises – big drama. But the article I read said one shortcut to assessing heart health was the number of full-body push-ups you could do (I don't know if this is true, but it motivated me!).

So there I had my clear, compelling reason.

I decided my trigger would be an alarm. It goes off every two hours between 10 am and 4 pm. I set it to remind me to be present and take a moment to focus on how I am feeling – tense, relaxed, excited, bored, etc. Being aware of my feelings leads me to a solution for improving my mood.

Without this method of checking in with myself, I tend to become absorbed in my work and completely lose sight of myself.

With this 2-hourly ritual in place, I chose to 'habit stack.' This is when you attach a new habit to an already established one. Every two hours, I would do ten push-ups to 40 or 50 push-ups daily. And as soon as they felt 'easy,' I would add another push-up to the cycle and slowly increment my way to 30 push-ups, non-stop.

This 'stacked' habit was a great micro habit because it did not take long to execute, and my reward was immediate upon completion – a sense of 'job done' and the enjoyment of feeling my chest and arms firm up as they filled with blood from the exercise.

I would always take a moment to remind myself I had made a choice, followed through, and was now reaping the benefits. A simple but effective celebration.

Now, I know what I am like. I have been known to start strong, but then 'life' gets in the way. And often legitimately so, like meetings or calls that overlap with the reminders. I decided when I started this plan to do two things. Firstly, encourage my son to do the same and hold me to account.

Secondly, I decided to treat any time I missed my goals as an isolated incident, with no guilt attached, and commit to doing the next session.

I also snoozed the alarm when it overlapped with a call or meeting so the reminder would not be lost if it went off at an inconvenient time. I quickly learned it is less annoying to do the exercise than to suffer interruptions from an alarm every eight minutes!

This is a small example but one that worked for me.

Here are three activities you can begin incorporating now to keep you moving toward your ultimate goals.

Step 1: The Power of the Positive

Having recognised your inner critic, get into the habit of telling it to shut up. Please do not be embarrassed. There's no need to say it out loud. But pay attention, and when you hear yourself being negative, shut that voice down. Do it every time you catch the critic in action.

Trust that it will eventually become submissive in response to your commands.

Next, begin drafting a few positive affirmations to replace those negative comments and give the unconscious mind new data to focus on. These are thoughtful, personal reflections that *you* create. Replacing negative thoughts with positive affirmations takes that negative energy and puts it to positive use.

If repeated often enough (by habit!), positive affirmations will eventually become encoded into our deepest evaluation of our self-worth.

On a sheet of paper, write something you would like to have or be in the future. It can be a material item or an idea, like creating more 'calm' in your life. Once you have identified your goal, write down three or more declarative statements about it. Declarative statements begin with "I."

For example, repeating, "I feel calm when stress arises" can help you regain focus, or "I have the talent to excel at this position" can increase your confidence during a job interview. Another great affirmation is "I am worthy of being/having _____." Then fill in the blank with whatever you are seeking. Create meaningful statements and repeat them to yourself whenever you can while continuing to quiet your inner critic.

Dr. Maxwell Maltz, the author of "Psycho Cybernetics," says it usually takes 21 days to notice a perceptible change in one's mental image. When you think about it, that is an amazingly short period to overcome a lifetime of negativity.

Step 2: Seeing is Believing: The Power of Visualisation

Did you know that you already use visualisation practically every day? Daydreaming, fantasising, and rehearsing situations in your mind are all forms of visualisation. Rather than expending vital energy replaying fears repeatedly, instead imagine the things you most desire; let them take shape in your mind, planting crucial mental seeds that subtly begin to align your feelings, thoughts, and actions.

Just as positive affirmations can counteract the inner critic's negative chatter, visualising something you deeply desire will plant the possibility firmly inside you. While brushing your teeth, walking to and from your car, or before falling asleep, focus your mind on something you desperately want and see yourself having it.

Orison Swett Marden, the American journalist who founded & edited *Success Magazine*, said, "We lift ourselves by our thought; we climb upon our vision of ourselves. If you want to enlarge your life, you must first enlarge your thoughts of it and of yourself. Hold the ideal of yourself as you long to be, always, everywhere—your ideal of what you long to attain—the ideal of health, efficiency, success (and fulfilment – added by me!!)."

Focus on what you *want* rather than what you do not want so your passions, goals, and desires start to take physical form in your daily life.

Step 3: Put It All Together

The last step in bringing your goals into your everyday awareness is to create a visual reminder of them.

Some call this a dream book or dream board. Begin looking for visual representations of what you want—material possessions, states of mind, career-related aspirations, etc.—and paste them onto a poster board. Be sure to uncover any underlying needs that specific material possessions might represent, such as a beach house symbolising a greater need for calm or relaxation. While turning your focus toward attaining material possessions is fine at some level, the motivation is more powerful when you fully understand the reasons behind that desire.

I say this because our need for 'things' is insatiable. I remember many years ago when I was at university. I could not conceive of how people spent tens of thousands of dollars each year when I could live a decent life as a student on less than $4,000 at the time.

Only a few years later, I was earning more than ten times that amount, then another 50%, and quite quickly more than double that again. Despite further significant salary increases throughout my career, more was always needed (or maybe I should say wanted!).

And there is also a part of me that could never be satisfied by material possessions. So set your goals on more than just 'things' so that your whole being is fulfilled, not just a part of you.

This may sound strange, but your talents are not just for your benefit. They are for the good of those around you, those you serve. There is no significance to be found in pleasing only yourself. I truly believe it is impossible to be selfish and truly significant.

Back to your dream board. Having completed this exercise, place your dream board where you will see it daily. Next to your bathroom mirror or on/in your wardrobe is typically a good idea. The back of a bathroom door is often a prime spot too – you can easily work out why…..

Once you are regularly repeating your personal affirmations and creating positive visualisations daily, your dream board is the final reinforcement that binds them all together.

Using these tools, you gradually align your thoughts, feelings, and actions toward achieving your greatest desires. Reflect again on Mohammad Ali's quote and add good mental habits to your will to succeed, making your goals all the more possible.

> "Act as if you have already achieved your goal, and it is yours."
> **— Dr. Robert Anthony, psychologist**

Dig deeper…

1. **"The Miracle Morning: The Not-So-Obvious Secret Guaranteed to Transform Your Life (Before 8AM)" by Hal Elrod**
   - This book introduces a life-changing morning routine that incorporates positive affirmations, visualisation, and other empowering practices.

2. **"Year of Yes: How to Dance It Out, Stand In the Sun and Be Your Own Person" by Shonda Rhimes (2015)**

- Shonda Rhimes shares her transformative experience of saying "yes" to unexpected opportunities, which leads to significant personal growth and a more positive outlook on life.

3. **"The Effect of Self-Affirmation on Social Cognition: A Meta-Analysis" (2019) by Lisa Legault et al., Published in 'Personality and Social Psychology Review'**

    - This comprehensive meta-analysis evaluates the effects of self-affirmation on social cognition, providing insights into its efficacy.

4. **"Rising Strong: How the Ability to Reset Transforms the Way We Live, Love, Parent, and Lead" by Brené Brown**

    - Brené Brown explores the power of resilience, discussing how facing adversity with a positive mindset can lead to personal growth and transformation.

5. **"Positive affirmations as a means of thinking about the self" by Christopher J. Armitage et al., Published in 'Journal of Health Psychology'**

    - This study investigates the psychological mechanisms through which positive affirmations can influence personal attitudes and behaviours, with a focus on health contexts.

6. **"Big Magic: Creative Living Beyond Fear" by Elizabeth Gilbert**

    - Elizabeth Gilbert delves into the importance of living a life driven by curiosity rather than fear, encouraging a positive and creative approach to life's challenges and opportunities.

CHAPTER 4.
VISIONARY THINKING MEETS PRACTICAL ACTION

"You only get what you plan to do. What you plan to do is where your priorities are. Where your priorities are is where your heart is. Where your heart is you will be effective in building your treasure."
— **Dan Brent Burt**

*In order to share one's true brilliance,
one initially has to risk looking like a fool"*
— **Criss Jami, Venus in Arms**

It is mid-1985, and I am running an errand for my mother.

Growing up, we never had a car, so we walked everywhere or used public transport. These days, particularly in New Zealand, that sounds like a huge inconvenience. Growing up in London, with good transport infrastructure and a lack of funds, it was common to move around the city this way.

My mother's approach to shopping was slightly unusual: to know every shopkeeper in the vicinity personally, do her shopping, and then send her fit young boys to bring that shopping home. I had two brothers - one older, one younger.

I won't lie – I was not too fond of this task, partly because it could be hard work but also because Mother sometimes had this wheeled contraption which, when seen in my possession, would signal immediate death to any street credibility I might have.

Only worse was the sense of letting my mother down or having to deal with the consequences if I tried to refuse. For those raised by Nigerian parents, you know exactly what I mean!!

I had recently finished a course in Computer Studies and was thinking about what to do next. My results needed to be stronger and relevant to the study of Law, which would have been my preference. Instead, I chose accountancy.

You may recall in the introduction to this book that I left school with no qualifications in Math. Some of that was due to a definite lack of talent in this area; most of it was due to a complete lack of application. Whatever the cause, the outcome was the same.

This was my first time choosing a long-term goal (at least three years of study and a minimum of 5 years post-qualification). When I mentioned this to my parents, they were delighted. As the child of Nigerian immigrants, they wanted a lawyer, doctor, teacher, accountant, or minister of religion. Box ticked!

However, I did come across my first obstacle quite quickly when an uncle of mine said, "You love words, and you love to argue. You should be a lawyer. With your history in Math, you have no chance of becoming an accountant."

Thanks, uncle!

I worked out I needed to do two things. Firstly, identify the steps I would take in the short term to keep me moving towards my goal. Secondly, to keep my eyes on the longer-term prize of passing my accountancy exams, obviously a field in which I had little talent.

I realised discipline would play a huge part in any success, the ability to stay on track when it gets difficult. I knew this journey was going to be tough, so I decided to get used to 'toughing it out.' Which takes us back to the shopping....

We had a tiny general store about 10-12 minutes' walk from home. Mum would shop there frequently and then ask us to collect the shopping. Often (thank God!), the purchase would not require the wheeled contraption, so we would carry the bags home in our hands.

However, that caused a different problem because ergonomic design was not at the forefront of people's minds when these plastic bags were manufactured. They were designed to be strong - and they were. The fact that, when weighted down with product, they cut into your hands like sharpened scissors was just the price you paid for such a robust solution.

But that's where the gold was!

I decided, between starting my undergraduate accounting qualifications and finishing the computer studies program, I would carry the bags home, every time, without stopping or adjusting my grip. This was a personal discomfort or endurance test.

I never told anyone what I was doing and have never shared this story up till now. I just knew I had to prove to myself that I could do more than I had previously done and that suffering, pain, challenges, or upsets would not get in the way of achieving my goal.

This was a small win, but looking back, it was the first step before moving on to bigger, more effective tools to deliver short-term actions that would add up to the desired, long-term results.

So, what do you really want to achieve in life? Anything is possible when you set your mind to it.

Note, it helps to be passionate about the direction you want to go in. People who are passionate about their lives and work tend to be more confident, creative, and successful. They inspire those around them, and their passion affects how they approach even the smallest tasks.

Even more than passion I would focus on another P word – perseverance. Most of your competitors, naysayers, critics, fans, whoever, are going to give up. If you keep putting one foot in front of the other and don't stop, you'll get there. And 'they' won't, not because you are that different but because you choose not to stop. You refuse to let your circumstances - or how you feel - determine what you do.

Just keep going.

Now, I haven't completely set passion aside. I do believe it is important because achieving a goal doesn't necessarily lead to fulfilment. I clearly recall a story from the famous actor Jim Carrey who talked about being broke one minute and wealthy the next.

It took about 6 months for him to realise that you can be every bit as miserable with a pile of cash than without it – especially when you realise that what you thought was going to make life great doesn't when you've finally got it.

Achieving goals is a mechanical process. Being fulfilled requires intention, like passion.

I have developed a little formula:

Passion + measured action = FULFILMENT

When you are passionately engaged in an activity, time flies by. What feels like five minutes can be five hours. It is something that is engrossing and allows you to forget yourself. You might even need to remember to eat or sleep. There's no time left for boredom and self-doubt when you follow your passion and work toward achieving your goals.

So, how do you find your passion? You may have several natural abilities that come to you easily, but that doesn't necessarily mean they're your passion. Take time to recall activities that were totally absorbing for you at any age.

Consider activities that engrossed you as a child when you were allowed to explore the world with fresh eyes and far fewer expectations. Ask family members and loved ones who have known you for some time to name some of the activities you were engaged in when they saw you at your happiest.

Go back to the Values and Purpose clarification exercise for further clues.

If you do not feel charged by an idea, it is wrong, and I would encourage you to continue digging deeper. Tapping into your passions, no matter how dormant they are, should leave you feeling enthusiastic, buzzing with excitement and possibilities.

VISIONARY THINKING MEETS PRACTICAL ACTION

Think about it for a while. Be compassionate with yourself —trust that it is there, and you will recognise it once you find it.

Once you have identified a few possibilities, consider why they excite you.

- What aspects of your personality do they spark?
- Does this activity give you a sense of independence, an opportunity to think creatively, or a chance to develop solutions?
- Does it allow you to interact with others, or is the quiet and solitude energising you?
- Do people praise you for your ability or tell you that you have a special touch or flair?

As you think about activities that engross you, write down the attitudes, behaviours, and skills necessary to accomplish them. All of this is critical information that will assist you in uncovering your unique combination of skills and abilities that support your passions.

Consider what you want to pursue once you have identified your passion(s). What do you want to achieve concerning your passion(s)? Then ask yourself *why* this particular achievement matters to you. Is this something that has deep, personal significance?

A warning; be sure you can distinguish your passion from something you've been told to value.

Imagine this scenario: I'm a coach who has typically worked one-on-one, but then I decide to jump into the world of team dynamics. It was like stepping into a new space, not entirely unknown but full of unexplored corners. This shift began with a corporate team that was, frankly, a bit of a mess. They were all over the place.

So, here's what I did first. I sat down with each team member, trying to get a handle on their viewpoints. This was my short-term plan: get to know the players on the field. It was a bit like being a detective, piecing together the clues of their office dynamics.

The long-term strategy? That was about bringing these individual stories together. I introduced something I called 'conflict resolution circles.' It's a simple idea – get everyone in a room, lay all the cards on the table, and really listen to each other. It's a little like those community meetings in stories, where everyone works together to solve the village problems.

Here's where it gets interesting. Over time, these sessions started to change the game. Conflicts became opportunities for innovation, and projects that were once a slog turned into team missions. The atmosphere in the office did a complete 180 – it was like breathing life back into a deflated balloon.

But this journey was more than just fixing a team. It was about seeing the bigger picture. Each person's goals and the team's objectives weren't just running parallel; they were interwoven and where appropriate, interdependent.

This whole experience was a solid reminder that teams are like intricate networks, each connection vital. Shifting my focus in coaching didn't just change my methods; it transformed my perspective on teamwork – and the importance of a clear roadmap to help navigate you to your end goals.

The next step I'd suggest is to make a plan and set some goals that will lead to achieving your dream. Be sure to write them down; there are good, scientific reasons for doing so which I will touch on now.

Writing goals down may require additional work on top of generating the goals. I promise you. It's worth the extra effort.

Firstly, it provides you with external (to your mind) storage. So, if you have your goals written where you are likely to see them repeatedly over a day, access and review are easy and staring at something will make remembering it much easier.

Let me use the words of Mark Murphy, a renowned commentator, and CEO of Leadership IQ, to expand on this important topic.

"The second reason written goals are important is "encoding," the biological process by which the things we perceive travel to our brain's hippocampus where they're analysed. From there, decisions are made about what gets stored in our long-term memory and, in turn, what gets discarded. Writing improves

that encoding process. In other words, when you write it down, it has a much greater chance of being remembered.

Study after study shows you will remember things better when you write them down. Typically, subjects for these types of studies are students taking notes in class. However, one group of researchers looked at people conducting hiring interviews.

When the interviewers took notes about their interviews with each candidate, they could recall about 23% more nuggets of information than those who didn't take notes.

It's not just general recall that improves when you write things down. Writing it down will also improve your recall of the essential information. You know how when you're in a classroom setting, there's some stuff the teacher says that's really important (i.e., it'll be in the test), and then there's the not-so-important (i.e., it won't be in the test). Well, one study found that when people weren't taking notes in class, they remembered just as many unimportant facts as important ones (there's a recipe for a "C").

But when people were taking notes, they remembered many more important facts and many fewer unimportant facts (and that, my friends, is the secret of "A" students). Writing things down doesn't just help you remember; it makes your mind more efficient by helping you focus on the truly important stuff. And your goals absolutely should qualify as truly important stuff."

Here is the ultimate test of a written goal:

"My goal is so vividly described in written form (including pictures, photos, drawings, etc.) that I could show it to other people, and they would know exactly what I'm trying to achieve."

Continuing our journey may feel overwhelming if you aim to accomplish something in an arena where you have yet to gain prior experience. No problem. Just remember, reading or talking with people who have travelled a similar path is always a good idea. You can get some great insights and see the truth in the statement, "A journey of 1,000 miles starts with the first step."

Once you have identified your true passions, they will invigorate you, and your excitement will give you the energy to get up earlier, stay up later, learn something new, or take whatever actions may be necessary to achieve your dreams.

You'll notice I talk about dreams, not just goals. When we were kids, it was nothing to dream. Then school, family, and friends trained us how not to. But we only have one shot at life – why not dream and head in that direction?

If you can, identify one meaningful reason not to dream and go for it and stop reading now. Go back to your "almost certain, probable future." But before you do that, I want to make an important point; the possibility of failure is no reason not to start – but failure is guaranteed if you don't start.

More importantly, failure is how you will get there. You will fail and get things wrong - fix them - and keep moving towards your goal.

See what I'm doing? I'm stalling you because I really don't want you to stop 😊

I once heard the story of a man who had a childhood dream of owning a bookstore. He grew up and put aside his dream, instead working at a corporate job to earn enough money to care for his family. However, he still occasionally daydreamed about what he'd name his store and what it would look like. But he never paid much attention to his daydreams.

In his mid-forties, he struggled with depression and could not understand his feelings. He made an offhand remark about his old childhood fantasy during therapy treatments. His therapist made a simple but wise suggestion. She asked him why he could not start selling used books out of his garage on the weekends. He did, and this simple step helped him to realise a lifelong dream.

Many of us are "all-or-nothing" thinkers. While our daydreams and fantasies hold the seeds of our most honest desires, we do not necessarily have to start by exactly replicating what is in our mind's eye. Rather, begin the process and hold fast to the ultimate goal.

The physical form it takes initially is less important and can evolve. The important thing is to start!

> "In life, the first thing you must do is decide what you really want. Weigh the costs and the results. Are the results worth the costs? Then make up

your mind completely and go after your goal with all your might."
—Alfred Montapert, author

Dig deeper....

1. **"How to Begin: Start Doing Something That Matters"** by Michael Bungay Stanier - A practical guide to identify and set clearly defined goals and make commitments while developing the resources and building the momentum to reach them.

2. **"Fast Forward: 5 Power Principles to Create the Life You Want in Just One Year"** by Wendy Leshgold and Lisa McCarthy - Offers methods to create a clear vision of the future, overcome limiting beliefs, and make steady progress toward big and bold goals.

3. **"Creating Your Best Life: The Ultimate Life List Guide"** by Caroline Adams Miller and Michael Frisch - Combines positive psychology and the science of goal accomplishment to achieve life fulfilment , happiness, and success.

4. **"Goals! How to Get Everything You Want Faster Than You Ever Thought Possible"** by Brian Tracy - Provides methods for practical goal setting and achieving, with a focus on capturing goals, planning, and daily work towards them.

5. **"All It Takes Is a Goal: The 3-Step Plan to Ditch Regret and Tap Into Your Massive Potential"** by Jon Acuff - Encourages taking action and seeing quick results through a three-step plan focusing on escaping the comfort zone and living in the potential zone.

6. **"Your Best Year Ever"** by Michael Hyatt - A research-driven system for setting and working toward goals, offering a five-step approach to goal setting and achievement.

CHAPTER 5.
OWNING YOUR JOURNEY

"The trouble with not having a goal is that you can spend your life running up and down the field and never scoring."
—Bill Copeland, Australian athlete

"Discipline is the bridge between goals and accomplishments."
— Jim Rohn, American business philosopher & motivational speaker

I have loved football (soccer) for as long as I can remember. And I was always good at it, a natural talent from God.

I even played football semi-professionally for a few years, after I qualified as an accountant. I always cherished the camaraderie of being in a team, helping to build links between disparate groups of people, alliances formed that were greater in total than the sum of the individual parts.

I have always wanted to be part of a story where dedication, determination, and desire combine to outweigh our competition's superior skills or talent. More on this below.

Interestingly, if you add curiosity to this potent mix, it can make for an unstoppable business, but that's a different conversation.....

I enjoyed playing in the semi-professional leagues, but my real joy was competing in the more social Sunday competitions, which, at the national level, was every bit as competitive. In England at the time, if you successfully won your city's knockout cup - and you could raise funds or secure the right sponsorships - you could enter the Football

Association's National Sunday Cup, a knockout competition to identify the best team in the country.

We had an unusual mix of talented guys. Everyone in the squad played semi-professional football, and we also had a few ex-professionals. A mix of teachers, plumbers, builders, firefighters, executives, entrepreneurs, and more we were 'all in', fully committed, and extremely confident.

And we decided, after more than 25 years of the club's existence, we would commit to winning the National Cup - 'The Nash' as we called it.

This was a serious commitment because, on top of Sunday games, our semi-professional obligations would see us playing in a match or training a further two times each week, 90 minutes on each occasion. The risk of injuries, or just plain fatigue, was high. But we were drawn to this goal, having reached the quarter-finals the year before and narrowly losing to the team who went on to win the tournament.

I had never committed to a national-level goal before. And to make the challenge even more difficult, we lost some key players. One of our mates transitioned to the professional ranks and, as a result, was no longer allowed to participate in this competition. So, working out how to progress two stages further in the competiton with gaps in key positions was daunting.

But someone had to win it. Why not us?

Long story short, we won. And I scored a goal in our 2-0 cup final victory!! Here's what I learned through this experience:

- You're going to be thinking anyway, why not think big?
- The goal should be scary as well as exciting. If it is linked to my passion, I'll keep going when others stop.
- Telling others (or committing along with others) increased my resolve.
    - I believe our highest role is in serving others. I knew my dream was inextricably linked to my teammates' and I didn't want to let them down.

- To stay on track, I only had to do one thing – the next right thing. And if I stayed focused on that, in the light of my goal, I made progress easier than I expected.

- Be patient. The tough times pass….they are a season, not a permanent state.

- The journey is every bit as good as the destination. Enjoy the small beginnings, each milestone, and who you become.

- Be accountable for everything – that means you can do something about it.
  - This may seem extreme, but I look at every situation in a binary way; you're accountable, or you're a victim. You can soothe yourself by trying to find some middle ground, but you'll be wasting energy concocting excuses instead of finding ways through, around, over, or under your challenges.

Some thoughts on accountability follow from a good friend of mine, Jonathan Stanley.

Jonathan Stanley's – accountability model

- I am accountable because I caused the problem.

- I am accountable because someone who works/ plays or is somehow connected with me caused the problem.

- I am accountable because circumstances have conspired to make me accountable.

- I am accountable because I have committed to doing whatever it takes. And whatever the problem, there's ALWAYS something I can do to move me in the right direction.

Staying with the theme of accountability but this time in the field of science, the story of Marie Curie stands out as a beacon of goal-setting, accountability, and overcoming obstacles.

Marie Curie, a Polish-born physicist and chemist, faced formidable challenges in her journey. In an era when women were seldom seen in the sciences, she broke through every barrier with unwavering determination. Battling financial limitations and societal scepticism, she pursued her research with relentless dedication.

Her groundbreaking work on radioactivity not only earned her two Nobel Prizes in Physics and Chemistry, making her the first woman to receive a Nobel Prize and the only person to win in two different scientific fields, but also paved the way for future advancements in medicine and science.

Curie's tenacity in the face of adversity, her commitment to her scientific goals, and her ability to hold herself accountable to her vision serve as a powerful example of how enduring dedication to one's goals can lead to extraordinary achievements, far beyond the immediate scope of their work.

The final word on accountability belongs to Nick Vujicic, an Australian American who was born without limbs (literally, no arms or legs) and has gone on to create a life that most would describe as extraordinary by any standards.

Watch the video called "No arms, no legs, no worries." This is inspiration of the highest order where you will see the living embodiment of accountability or a no-excuses mentality. Enjoy!!

https://www.youtube.com/watch?v=vAVbMggSU48

Back to soccer as we head towards the close of this chapter. When I played soccer at a higher level, I never trained as hard as I should, and being six foot three tall and heavy-boned, I was prone to injuries.

During this push for the trophy, I badly strained my back, causing me to miss a few games. On the advice of the club physio, I saw an osteopath. The treatments were a revelation to me, and each manipulation brought its own relief. But I would be back to square one after each subsequent game.

The solution? For the run-up to the final, I went to the osteopath twice between games, stopped participating in training for fear of aggravating the injury, and stepped onto the field only for competitive games.

The easy option would have been to stop. I carried half of the costs of these treatments and had to travel for up to an hour each way to see the osteopath. But the prize of winning this competition and not letting my teammates down just drove me on. I wanted to be of service to them and meet my own goals too.

This was sport. Your goal could be anything, but if you can attach it to being in service to someone or something else – friend, partner, child, team, or whoever – there will be another unshakeable dimension to your determination to hit the mark.

Recent findings in the field of positive psychology offer compelling insights into the power of goal-setting. Dr. Martin Seligman of the University of Pennsylvania, a leading figure in this domain and also famous for his work in the area of 'learned helplessness', has conducted extensive research showing that individuals who set and actively pursue personal goals exhibit higher levels of long-term happiness and psychological well-being.

This is corroborated by studies from the University of California, which found that goal-directed actions contribute to a sense of purpose and fulfilment in life.

These insights not only align with my personal experiences on the soccer field but also resonate with the stories of countless individuals who have found joy and satisfaction in pursuing their passions and achieving their aspirations.

Incorporating such scientifically validated information into our understanding of goal-setting transforms it from mere anecdote to a compelling proposition that is grounded in empirical evidence.

What is a goal? How do you set good ones?

Webster's New World Dictionary defines a goal as "an end one strives to attain." Achieving your goals requires you to devise a strategy and undertake specific actions to achieve the desired result.

Making a specific plan is the very next step, and by having a set plan, you are organising the actions you'll take toward achieving your dreams.

Dr. Philip E. Humbert, writer, speaker, and success coach, says that in identifying goals and coming up with a game plan for achieving them, the goals should be tested against the following criteria: specific, simple, significant, strategic, rational, tangible, written, shared, and *consistent with your core values.*

Setting goals is about more than just being the right thing to do. Setting goals will help you:

- Disseminate the workload more evenly
- Assess your progress along the way
- Help you figure out how to move forward if you encounter drawbacks
- Manage your time more effectively
- Establish what you are trying to accomplish
- Clarify the definition of success; and
- Develop a clear purpose that can help you recruit support and encouragement from others.

Long-term goals are critical, but we often do not progress as a result of being too focused on today and tomorrow because that is clearer than what could happen next month or next year.

This is technically described as 'cognitive tunneling,' when you focus on the easiest task because you're overwhelmed by the options available.

Other reasons for not progressing with long-term goals include the following:

- Fear of starting, generally related to perfectionism.
- This is where the statement' *progress, not perfection'* comes into its own. Forward momentum of any kind is better than no momentum. Just start and remove the excuses.
- Fear of failure – which is almost always related to what others think. This means you give the power to determine your future to people you don't know, who aren't particularly thinking about

you, don't have your best interests at heart, and almost certainly do not care to do what you're doing. Really?

- Fear of success which is not necessarily about the end result but probably the journey.

- As a huge proponent of *Stephen Covey's 7 Habits of Highly Effective People*, he recognises "private victories always precede public victories". In simple terms, this means making and keeping promises to ourselves precedes making and keeping promises to each other.

  - If you are going to achieve your most meaningful goals, expect it to be hard work because you will need to change a lot to get there. Of course, the answer is to see the journey as part of your success, a key aspect of fulfilment.

Finally – commit to the process, not just the goal.

Below are different tools for overcoming obstacles and staying laser-focused on your dreams.

Use the W.O.O.P. strategy for results.

What's W.O.O.P. strategy? I'll tell you…..

- **W**ish – what, exactly, do you want?
- **O**utcome – what would the outcome be of achieving this wish?
- **O**bstacles (hurdles!) – what will get in the way of achieving this outcome?
- **P**lan - how will you work through these obstacles?

S.M.A.R.T. goals

You can also ensure you are on the right path with your goals by using the acronym "**S. M.A.R.T.**" Get a fresh sheet of paper and write the following words:

Specific

Measurable

Achievable

Relevant; and

Timescaled

We'll come back to this shortly.

As stated previously, the key to setting attainable, relevant goals is to see your dream and imagine it happening, then take steps to achieve your results. That can seem overwhelming if you are attempting to achieve something you've never done, which is usually the case.

To assist you, I will give you a technique to create a detailed blueprint for achieving your dream. It may seem a bit *"airy fairy"* or *"woo woo"* but just give it a go and see what happens.

Here's step 1: Imagine reaching the goal you wrote down. Close your eyes and see it happening. Where are you? What are you wearing? Who is with you? What are the smells? What body sensations are you feeling? What are your emotions?

Really feel and see it all happening right now. Write all this down in your notebook so you can refer to it again and again.

Now take step 2: Once you have that clear vision of your accomplishment, think about what came just before that moment and then what came just before that, and just before that, all the way back to the present. Write this all down in your project notebook. You can break it down by hours, days, or weeks, but the more detailed you are, the easier it will be to proceed. This may take you a few days or a few weeks. That's OK. It is more important to take your time and be detailed about the dream you want to pursue.

"A goal clearly defined is a goal half attained." Carl Jones

Step 3: Go back through what you wrote in your notebook and identify all the short-term goals and actions you met to turn your dream into reality. When you write out your main goals, be sure to take note of the ways they account for each of the "SMART" attributes:

First, be as **Specific** as possible. For example, which gives you a clearer picture: "Make more money" or "Increase my weekly income by $100 by December 15, 2023"? Certainly, the latter is much more specific and is a good example of the way to write your goals for maximum success.

Just saying, "I will increase my income by $100," isn't enough. You must be specific, saying $100 per what: Per day? Per week? Per month? Per year? And then add *by when* that will happen.

Next, make sure the goals are **Measurable**. Using the above example, you can measure your increased income each week.

If your ultimate goal is to run in a marathon and your short-term goal is to run five miles a day, that is measurable. But it is even better if you can say how long it will take you to run those five miles; for example, "I will run five miles in 45 minutes each day beginning June 18." This keeps you informed of how you're doing.

When you work out at a gym, some places offer you a grid sheet where you can keep track of the number of repetitions and the amount of weight you use on each machine. If you have ever used that system, you know how motivating it can be to see your progress over time.

Whatever your goal is, physical or otherwise, create the same type of grid to track your progress.

Third, you want your goal to be **Achievable**. And bear in mind achievable does not equal easy.

Who is to say whether a goal is achievable? Only you. But you want to ensure you haven't left out any smaller goals to get to the bigger one. If your goal is to be a pilot of jumbo jets, there are many steps you must go through to get there, especially if you've never flown a plane before. That's why backward visioning (from the end goal back to today) is so powerful; it keeps you in tune with the smaller, attainable goals you must reach for your big dream.

Fourth, your goal should be **Relevant** to your broader objective without equating relevant with *reasonable*. Choosing reasonable goals only leads to reasonable outcomes, which are unlikely to equate to achieving your dreams.

Relevance is also important so you don't end up in the dilemma Stephen Covey describes where you are making great progress in the wrong direction or worse still, on the wrong goals.

At risk of repeating myself, people will always tell you that your goal is stupid, can't be done (at all or by you) etc. The same was said about flying, telephones, televisions, radios, cars, computers, electricity, and almost every innovative, life-changing thing ever created.

Before the puzzle was solved, they were all unreasonable goals. Just make sure you set up those simple, short-term goals so you can keep on going and not get overwhelmed.

Finally, give yourself a **Timeframe** to achieve each goal. You can always extend the timeframe if needed, but a defined schedule will help you stay focused and on track. Just saying, "I will lose 10 pounds," isn't enough. You must say *when* you will complete your goal: "I will lose 10 lbs. by July 21."

By being as precise as possible, you further increase the likelihood of being able to attain your goals. Vague plans eat up time, energy, resources, and opportunity. Clearly defined plans allow for specific, straightforward navigation.

Chunking

Another tool for your toolkit is the technique of 'chunking,' where you break long-term goals into diarised, short-term tasks or 'chunks'. If you combine chunking with the discipline of 'time blocking' (some call it 'time boxing'), you have some powerful techniques for achieving your goals.

Time blocking is an act of discipline. It requires you to set a fixed amount of time for each task you will undertake and then put it in your schedule. You commence with the relevant task then do what you said you would, when you said you would do it.

Some of its major advocates, including Elon Musk and Bill Gates, have made this technique famous. It means you will have less unplanned free time, but if you limit your actionable next steps to things you can do in 30 minutes a day, finding time for things you are passionate about is always possible.

Regarding your long-term goals, I suggest working on them first thing in the morning. I know some of you will not be morning people, but you can more easily control how you spend your time at the start of your day. It is also when your willpower is at its greatest before dissipating over the course of the day.

Schedule your goals and decide in advance. Do your most meaningful work before you do anything else. This avoids decision fatigue which occurs when you are tired of making choices and then choose to do what's easy - like not exercising or eating unhealthy food, even though you want to lose weight. That's one for me!

Motivation is good. Discipline is preferable and predictable.

We have already noted it is good to consider possible hurdles and design approaches for overcoming them. This way, your subconscious mind would already have done a deal of work addressing issues and will be fixed on resolving them because you made that decision long ago.

Here's another tool you can play with to identify what is most effective for you. It's called the "if/ then" strategy to avoid the tyranny of the urgent or what psychologists call *"urgency bias"*.

Basically, you focus on where you might stumble. Then you say, "If X happens, I will do Y ". As I said, decide beforehand and let your subconscious prepare for the challenges ahead.

Many years ago, I was trained in a project management methodology called Goal Directed Project Management or G.D.P.M. We had to identify the ultimate goal and work backward to the starting point today.

Recent research suggests that working back from a goal achieved increases the likelihood of achieving the planned goal. This is because solutions to obstacles are better understood when considered from the perspective of having overcome them.

A couple of examples follow so this doesn't just sounds like "words of wisdom from Sam" - a family joke that my kids will laugh about when they see this....

A study led by Jooyoung Park, an assistant professor in the Department of Management at Peking University HSBC Business School, investigated the impact of different planning methods on goal pursuit. The research found that for complex tasks, backward planning — where you start from the end goal and work your way back to the present — allowed participants to more clearly anticipate necessary steps and stick to their original plan. This approach led to higher expectations for reaching goals and a reduction in feelings of time pressure. This study suggests that changing the way of constructing plans can produce different outcomes, particularly in academic and career contexts. Participants who used backward planning felt more motivated and less anxious, with increased confidence and more effortful actions.

Another study, highlighted in an article from Psychology Today, discusses the concept of self-control fatigue and how it relates to achieving goals. The study, based on the work of willpower psychologist Roy Baumeister, found that self-control is a limited resource that can get depleted, much like a battery. However, focusing on the end goal can help replenish this resource. When individuals work on tasks they truly want to be doing, they are less likely to become depleted. This implies that keeping the end goal in mind can provide the motivation and energy needed to maintain self-control and persist in goal-directed behaviours.

These studies underscore the effectiveness of backward planning and keeping a clear end goal in mind for achieving complex tasks and long-term objectives. They also highlight the psychological aspects of goal pursuit, such as motivation, anticipation, and self-control.

The summary of this section is as follows; be clear about what you want, start with the end in mind, plan for obstacles, be disciplined with your time, and get comfortable being uncomfortable.

Try to drop perfectionism and fail your way to success. Take control of your emotions and redefine your feelings to your advantage.

A great example of this is the language the world-famous All Blacks rugby team uses. They replace the word 'pressure' or 'uncertainty' with 'excitement,' emphasising the positive.

The effectiveness of your action plan depends upon your preparation. Give yourself every advantage to succeed by gaining knowledge through books, jobs, or talking with experienced individuals. The fine detail of your dream might be unique to you, but the tools you will need along the way are certain to have been used by others.

Learn from their mistakes, not by repeating them.

For instance, if your goal is to get a job with a large corporate accounting firm and you have never studied accounting, you are more likely to achieve your goal by including the appropriate studies in your plan.

Planning to be lucky or working out that shortcut that removes the hard yards doesn't make sense. No one is saying this will be easy – just that it will be worth it.

Time for another formula:

Conduct (what) + purpose (why) = Integrity (how)

In this chapter I have used a few sporting analogies. From my experiences in team sports, I've grown to appreciate the integration of each individual's unique role and the collective strength of a united group into personal development concepts. This approach is shaped by an understanding that collaboration and support networks have a significant role in enhancing personal growth, complementing the emphasis on individual efforts found in traditional self-help methods.

From my perspective, the dynamics of teamwork in sports offer an insightful framework for self-improvement. It's not solely focused on the journey of individual resilience and self-discovery, but also on the power of interdependent roles and mutual support in achieving shared success. This view does not detract from the importance of personal effort; instead, it recognises the additional layers and depth that teamwork and community support contribute to reaching personal milestones and navigating life's hurdles (that word again!).

A closing point. Flexibility is key; shifting your plan to reflect new information or conditions is OK. Life evolves, and things change, so be prepared to adapt. If mistakes throw you off course, reformat your plan. After all, it is YOUR plan, no one else's. It has to work for YOU.

Always maintain a mental picture of achieving your goal, and make sure your plan is designed to get you from where you are now to where you ultimately want to be. Remain true to the elements of your plan that are working and revise those that are not; this will keep you on the most direct path to your final destination.

You've probably noticed a fair amount of self-discipline in goal-setting. Once you set a specific goal, establish a daily routine (or a habit ☺) of specific everyday tasks - no matter how small - to keep yourself on track.

This is why having daily visual reminders and rituals is so important. Setting aside time for reading, absorbing new content and looking at your dream board provides a powerful daily dose of motivation.

As Jim Rohn so eloquently said,

'self-discipline is the bridge between your goals and accomplishments".

Digging deeper....

1. **"Man's Search for Meaning" by Viktor Frankl:**
   - With over 16 million copies sold, Frankl's book is a profound exploration of finding purpose and setting life goals amidst extreme adversity, making it a classic in personal development literature.

2. **"Can't Hurt Me: Master Your Mind and Defy the Odds" by David Goggins:**
   - Goggins' memoir, detailing his journey of overcoming adversity to become a top endurance athlete, is a bestseller that has resonated with many for its insights on resilience and goal setting.

3. **"Extreme Ownership: How U.S. Navy SEALs Lead and Win" by Jocko Willink and Leif Babin:**

- This book by former Navy SEALs, focusing on leadership and personal accountability, has gained significant popularity, especially among those interested in military principles applied to personal development.

4. **"Life Without Limits: Inspiration for a Ridiculously Good Life" by Nick Vujicic:**
    - Nick Vujicic's inspiring story, based on his life without limbs, has captivated readers worldwide, offering lessons in overcoming physical and mental barriers.

5. **"Fast Forward: 5 Power Principles to Create the Life You Want in Just One Year" by Wendy Leshgold and Lisa McCarthy:**
    - This book, co-authored by Wendy Leshgold, encourages readers to create a clear vision of their future, overcome limiting beliefs, and make steady progress toward ambitious goals

CHAPTER 6.
RIDING THE "HABITS" WAVE TO SUCCESS

> *"Desire is the key to motivation, but it is determination and commitment to an unrelenting pursuit of your goal— a commitment to excellence— that will enable you to attain the success you seek."*
> **– Mario Andretti, race car driver**

While we were still dating, my wife and I decided two things. Firstly, we would have a big family. It would consist of biological children or a mix of our biological children and those we had adopted. In the end, we had five biological children. An awesome blessing – that felt like a curse on the odd occasion!!

And no, we didn't adopt after that lot arrived!

The second thing we agreed on was the world is too big a place to live your life in the same country.

Things were happening where we lived, which, combined with the mounting pressure of work and our likely future, caused us to explore moving overseas.

We thoroughly explored options in Europe, Australasia, and North America. We chose New Zealand and have never regretted our choice, although the distance from the UK can prove challenging.

Deciding to move abroad was about more than a new address; it was a craving to experience life through a new cultural lens. Living in different countries wasn't just a change of scene, it was a chance to walk in others' shoes and add new colours to our family's life. Each new culture we embrace opens our eyes to different ways of chasing dreams and living life, showing us that there's no single right way to do it.

Navigating the challenges of moving overseas, we tackled the essentials: paperwork, health checks, and liaising with officials. These tasks, while daunting, were crucial steps in our journey.

Making the decision was an achievement in itself, but once we were on that journey, it became increasingly difficult to sustain. At the time, our children ranged from 10 years old to a newborn baby.

Realising the complexity of our move, we sought professional help. This decision, an investment in our family's future, streamlined our transition and taught us the value of seeking expertise when needed.

How is this relevant? Let me introduce you to my concept of **'keep the kettle boiling'** strategies. These are the actions that keep you going when the going gets tough. But you don't have to do it alone. That help can be paid for or come from family and friends who'll see you through.

Identify your options before you need them. That way, you can plan (save?) for these moments and move through them seamlessly, minimising any interruption to your progress.

In this case, we reduced the time to apply for permanent residence in New Zealand by at least 50%. We were awarded permanent resident status while still in London in June 2005. We had a 12-month window to move to New Zealand, ending by the following June.

We arrived in New Zealand on 1 December 2005. Our move involved a whirlwind of activities – resignations, farewells, and packing. Each step, filled with emotion and excitement, marked our commitment to a new beginning.

Moving from the UK to New Zealand was my leap into a different way of life. Back in the UK, everything moved fast and followed a tight schedule. But in New Zealand, I found a more laid-back atmosphere, where life seemed more in sync with nature.

This change taught me to slow down, to savour moments instead of constantly chasing time. Adapting to this new lifestyle wasn't just about getting used to a new place; it was about rethinking my approach to personal growth. I began to see it as a natural journey, not a race. This experience reshaped my goals and how I work towards them, teaching me to embrace simplicity and a more balanced view of life.

Embracing New Zealand's unique cultural values and practices brought a refreshing perspective to my goal-setting and achievement methods. In a culture that values balance, I learned the importance of integrating work with well-being, leading me to set goals that aren't just career-focused but also enrich my overall quality of life.

The Kiwi (particularly the people indigenous Māori people's) emphasis on community and collective success taught me to consider how my goals could benefit not just myself but also those around me. This shift from a purely individualistic approach to a more communal one has been a game-changer, making my journey towards my goals more inclusive and fulfilling.

It's a perspective that I wouldn't have gained had I not stepped out of my comfort zone and immersed myself in a culture so different from what I was used to.

As we discussed, there are two primary aspects associated with goal setting; the first is creating realistic and compelling goals, and the second is developing a programme and lifestyle that supports them. If you haven't made a dream board (see Chapter 3) or written down your goals (Chapter 4), stop and do it right now!

As I mentioned earlier, research shows that forming a habit takes around 66 days. By not taking these steps, you're wasting valuable time!

Think of it this way: if you can maintain your new routine for around two months, you have a strong chance of success.

Another example from my experience. My fitness journey, starting with brief walks (thank you, Glenn Marvin) and culminating in a 50 km ultramarathon, demonstrates setting and achieving incremental goals.

Where do you find the inspiration to keep moving forward? The first step is establishing a positive daily routine that includes being mindful of your daily goals. Take a few minutes to reread your written goals and look at your dream board every morning and every night before you sleep.

Start and end your day on a positive note. This both sets up your day and makes your sleep time more productive. If you are wrestling with a problem, ask your mind to work on it while you sleep and give you some ideas when you wake. Then, be ready to capture your new ideas when you wake up.

"Value the journey, not just the goal" - Effective Daily Routine

Morning Routine:

1. **Wake Up Early:**
   - Set a consistent wake-up time that gives you ample time before your day's commitments begin.

2. **Hydration and Nutrition:**
   - Start with a glass of water.
   - Have a healthy breakfast to fuel your day (unless you're fasting)

3. **Mindful Meditation or Quiet / Prayer Time:**
   - Spend 10-15 minutes in prayer, meditation or quiet reflection to centre your thoughts.

4. **Physical Activity:**
   - Engage in at least 30 minutes of exercise (e.g., walking, yoga, gym workout).

5. **Review Your Goals:**
   - Take a few minutes to read through your goals and affirmations.

6. **Plan Your Day:**

- Prioritise your tasks using the Eisenhower Box (or Covey's Urgent/ Important quadrants).
- Allocate specific times for each task (time blocking)

Evening Routine:

1. **Digital Detox:**
   - Limit screen time at least 1 hour before bed.
2. **Reflect on the Day:**
   - Spend 10 minutes reflecting on what went well and what could be improved.
3. **Prepare for Tomorrow:**
   - Set out clothes, prepare meals, or organise work materials for the next day.
4. **Relaxation Time:**
   - Engage in a relaxing activity like reading, listening to calming music, or a hobby.
5. **Gratitude Journal:**
   - Write down three things you were grateful for today.
6. **Sleep Hygiene:**
   - Go to bed at a consistent time in a dark, cool, quiet environment to ensure quality sleep.

Time Management Tips:

- **Use Time Blocking:** Allocate specific blocks of time for different activities or tasks.
- **Limit Multitasking:** Focus on one task at a time for better productivity and quality.
- **Use Covey's Urgent/ Important Quadrants:** Focus your efforts on the things that will give the greatest long-term benefits. See Appendix 3 for more details.

Prioritisation Techniques/ Tips:

- **Must, Should, Could Method:** Classify tasks into 'must do', 'should do', and 'could do' categories.
- **Pareto Principle (80/20 Rule):** Focus on the 20% of tasks that will yield 80% of the results.
- **Daily Top 3:** Each morning, identify the top three tasks that are critical for that day.

Meditation or mindfulness is a great way of simultaneously relaxing and awakening the mind, creating focus. A simple morning meditation involves sitting comfortably (cross-legged on the floor or a bed or chair) with your back upright and your hands open, palms down on your knees. Pay attention to the inhalation and exhalation of your breath.

During this time, thoughts are bound to enter your mind. Clearing the mind of thoughts is challenging. I manage it briefly at times, though the benefits aren't entirely clear to me. When thoughts come, notice them, don't judge them, then let them go and return to focusing on your breathing.

Then take out your goals and, read them over, look at your dream board. Your mind is open and receptive after meditation, allowing you to absorb your goals and think of new tasks or activities to move your projects forward.

Another option is to wake up 20 minutes earlier and read something inspirational or write in a journal. Personal development coach and professional motivator John Di Lemme is a staunch advocate of beginning your day with an inspirational exercise:

> *"A daily cornerstone for me is spending 45-60 minutes each morning exercising and absorbing a motivational message. This habit warms me up for the day ahead. Everyone washes their physical body....... but 95% of people will find an excuse about why they cannot find the time to invest in the habit of feeding their minds!"*

Reading the works of great motivators, spiritual leaders, or biographies of notable historical people can fill you with positive energy and help you focus on bigger-picture concerns. With the advent of Audible, Spotify, and other digital platforms, excuses for not 'reading' more books are thinner than ever.

Listen to other positive messages, helpful books, or inspirational music during your morning commute or daily errands.

Tom Chi is an American inventor, coach, speaker, and investor. He tells an interesting story. Chi rose quickly to very senior roles in organisations like Google, Microsoft, and Yahoo, to name a few. He credited much of his progress to his girlfriend at the time, who had secured a place in graduate business school which gave him access to the study materials.

He would listen to them on the way to work, and what he learned he would apply at work. Then he would listen to them again on the way home to see if he had any new insights, having tried out what he learned.

He continually experimented, refined, and then reapplied his learnings. It was, he says, what set him apart and underpinned his meteoric rise.

You'll find that the more room you make for personal development, the easier it will be to manage any outside negativity. Minimise contact with anyone who doubts or belittles your changes.

Or, if needs be, break contact with them completely even if it is just for a period. It's that important and the road is tough enough without having the additional burden of the negativity of unhelpful family or 'friends.'

Find a daily health or fitness program that suits you as part of your development plan. One of the upsides of Covid-19 is there are now so many free fitness programs that cater to every circumstance. They also recognise that participants may be suffering financially, so often, there will be zero cost attached to any required equipment, using items you already have at home.

Your fitness regime doesn't have to be detailed or complicated. My go-to exercise for staying fit these days is walking. I do this at pace, at least five times a week for up to 4.5 hours once a week. When I started, my walks lasted about 20-30 minutes, but the benefits of de-stressing, thinking, and overall improvements in energy led me to do more and more.

The main point about developing a daily routine is that you always keep your goals in front of you. Taking action every day, no matter how small, towards completing one of your short-term goals will lead you closer and closer to achieving your dreams.

In the book 'The One Thing' Gary Keller encourages the reader to answer this question daily:

'What is the one thing I could do today that would make all other tasks either easy or unnecessary?

Of course, this activity would have to be identified in the light of your ultimate goal. But remember what I said earlier, I only had to do one more thing each day to stay on track with my ultimate goal.

Try these additional action steps to support you in achieving your goals each of which can become a new habit:

- Arrange a meeting with a friend or colleague you admire once a month and report progress.
- Limit TV, social media, or other activities and spend time learning about others who have succeeded in your field of interest.
- Learn from their mistakes rather than making the same mistakes as them.
- Choose one or two activities you can realistically incorporate into your life and break them into three-month timelines.
- Once you've developed the desired habit for three months, expand on it by choosing a complementary or related activity, and then incorporate that for the next three months.

Remember to allow for setbacks. If you can't meet your goal that week, prioritise that activity during the following week. Also, refer back to some of the exercises outlined in this book—such as visualisation—to stay motivated.

By making the slightest positive change, you'll find that once you begin experiencing its benefits, you'll need less and less of the gratification you receive from old habits.

As the Dalai Lama says, "If you think small things don't make a difference, try spending a night in a room with a mosquito!"

Finally, take time to acknowledge your efforts and celebrate your successes. If you've begun to take steps toward meeting one of your goals, you're freeing yourself from anxiety and restlessness. Celebrate this progress. It is a form of positive reinforcement.

> *"Vision without action is merely a dream. Action without vision just passes the time. Vision with action can change the world."*
> **—Joel Barker, independent scholar, and futurist**

Dig deeper....

1. **"Atomic Habits: An Easy & Proven Way to Build Good Habits & Break Bad Ones" by James Clear:**
   - Clear's book is a comprehensive guide on forming good habits and breaking bad ones, emphasising the power of small, incremental changes.

2. **"The 7 Habits of Highly Effective People: Powerful Lessons in Personal Change" by Stephen R. Covey:**
   - This classic by Covey offers a principle-centered approach for achieving personal and professional effectiveness through character and ethics.

3. **"Drive: The Surprising Truth About What Motivates Us" by Daniel H. Pink:**
   - Pink explores the dynamics of motivation, revealing the mismatch between what science knows and what business does, and how that affects our lives.

4. **"Thinking, Fast and Slow" by Daniel Kahneman:**
   - Kahneman's book delves into the dual aspects of the mind and how they shape our decisions, offering insights into human rationality and irrationality.

5. **"Outliers: The Story of Success" by Malcolm Gladwell:**

- Gladwell examines the factors that contribute to high levels of success, offering an intriguing view on how external factors like timing, culture, and upbringing play a significant role.

CHAPTER 7.
HURDLE HOPPING: TURN OBSTACLES INTO OPPORTUNITIES

"Anytime you suffer a setback or disappointment, put your head down and plow ahead."
— **Les Brown, 21st century motivational speaker**

"I've failed over and over again in my life and that is why I succeed.... I'm strong enough as a person to face failure and move on. If I fail I won't feel bad. I can accept failure. What I will not accept from myself is not trying."
— **Michael Jordan, pro basketball legend**

My father died in November 1998, one month before the birth of our third daughter. In his later years, he grew weaker but never lost his inspiring spirit. This quote reminds me of him.

Strength does not come from physical capacity. It comes from an indomitable will." – Mahatma Gandhi.

Whatever obstacles were in his way - physical, financial, familial, emotional - he would take a breath and work out how to move forward without a word of complaint.

I remember while studying for my professional accountancy exams, I hit a wall. The complexities of financial regulations, advanced statistics and a pile of accounting standards felt insurmountable. I'd spend long nights at the local library, surrounded by textbooks and past papers, feeling increasingly overwhelmed.

Seeing me struggle, my father, who was very familiar with uphill battles, pulled me aside me one evening. He shared stories of his own personal challenges, reminding me that persistence was key. Considering the challenges he faced daily, this gave me a renewed sense of purpose.

Ultimately, I might not make it - but it wasn't going to be because I gave up!!

Dad was a relentless optimist and had a willing partner in my mum. No matter what we faced, they could see the bright side. So much of their resilience came from their faith, a real-life, practical set of principles and tools tested in the fire and proven worthy.

They also used humour to lighten even the darkest moments, a strategy I have come to use myself. This quote accurately reflects their attitude:

"If laughter cannot solve your problems, it will definitely DISSOLVE them, so you can think clearly about what to do about them."

I'd encourage you to try this. Begin each day with the 'Laugh at Life' exercise. Spend a few minutes thinking of something amusing or lighthearted – it could be a funny memory, a joke, or even a comical observation about life. Jot this down in a journal or on a Post It or on your phone.

Throughout the day, whenever you face a challenge or feel stressed, take a moment to read this and remind yourself to view life's hurdles with a sense of humour. This practice helps cultivate a mindset where laughter becomes a reflex, not just a reaction, easing your way through daily challenges.

My belief is obstacles are there to introduce you to your true character. Use them to your advantage.

Here's a powerful affirmation I use: *"Every challenge I face is an opportunity to grow and confirm my strengths"*.

Conventional wisdom often paints obstacles as mere hindrances, something to be avoided or swiftly overcome. My approach, however, sees them as invaluable teachers. Each challenge, rather than being a roadblock, is an opportunity for learning and self-discovery. Where others might see a barrier, I force myself to see a chance to grow, to adapt, and to uncover strengths I never knew I had.

While we are on the topic of character, I will share another brief story.

Growing up, my two closest relationships outside of my immediate family were with my favourite cousin Caleb (we called him 'K'), and my best friend, Ricky. K grew up in a family of five sisters, so he spent a lot of time at our place – a family of three boys!

Ricky also had two sisters at home and felt comfortable in a home of 3 boys. They saw a lot of my dad and became used to his wise ways and quiet influence.

> *Leadership is not about being in charge. It is about taking care of those in your charge." – Simon Sinek*

Dad's behaviour and approach to life made his disabilities seem irrelevant. I never fully understood this until I told Ricky my dad had passed away. His first reaction was one of shock, and he blurted out, 'The last time I saw your dad, he was well.'

Later it struck me that Ricky had never seen my dad when he was not paralysed on his right side, unable to work and provide for his family in the way he so desperately wanted to. Still, how he carried himself and his character made him well in others' eyes.

Years later, I read the book 'The Obstacle Is The Way" by Ryan Holiday. The basic premise of the book is captured in the title; rather than getting in the way of progress, obstacles mark the way of progress. Embrace them, and you will develop your character and identify the most direct route to your goal.

Further adding to the discussion of obstacles as pathways to growth is research on post-traumatic growth, a concept explored by psychologists Richard G. Tedeschi and Lawrence G. Calhoun. Their studies reveal that individuals who experience significant challenges often report increased personal strength, improved relationships, and a greater appreciation for life. This concept, detailed in their work 'Posttraumatic Growth: Conceptual Foundations and Empirical Evidence,' aligns with the narrative of my father's life – how his consistent battle with life's trials did not diminish him, but rather, enriched his character and outlook.

As touched on earlier, for years, my perspective on problems or obstacles was they arise to prevent me from ever getting to my end goal.

Then I became familiar with this gift of a quote and, over time, added further meaning to the potential reasons for obstacles.

Obstacles often reveal your inner strengths and prepare you for greater successes, rather than preventing you from reaching your goals.

Let me explain.

We have limited knowledge, so we can never know what would have happened without the challenges we face. Could not having to navigate the obstacle in front of me have resulted in a bigger, much stiffer challenge?

Could the obstacle be there to ensure that other activities or events align when I need them to? Have I avoided a fatal accident by addressing the issue, or am I going through these difficulties to benefit those who will follow?

These days I have decided that all obstacles are specifically for my benefit – I just might not be able to see how. But even if I can't, I know I will have to develop my character to overcome whatever the current obstacle is and, in so doing, become a better version of myself.

Many of you will know this fable. There was once a farmer who owned a horse and had a son. One day, his horse ran away. The neighbours came to express their concern: "Oh, that's too bad. How are you going to work the fields now?" The farmer replied: "Good thing, bad thing, who knows?"

In a few days, his horse returned and brought another horse with her. Now, the neighbours were glad: "Oh, how lucky! Now you can do twice as much work as before!" The farmer replied: "Good thing, bad thing, who knows?"

The next day, the farmer's son fell off the new horse and broke his leg. The neighbours were concerned again: "Now that he is incapacitated, he can't help you around; that's too bad." The farmer replied: "Good thing, bad thing, who knows?"

Soon, the news came that a war had broken out, and all the young men were required to join the army. The villagers were sad because they knew that many of the young men would not come back. The farmer's son could not be drafted because of his broken leg.

His neighbours were envious: "How lucky! You get to keep your only son." The farmer replied: "Good thing, bad thing, who knows?" You get the point.

People sometimes refer to this story as one where we are encouraged to stay present and not spend too much energy on trying to give meaning to what has happened, and there's value in this perspective.

But I understand this story differently, seeing that I could choose one of the options every time and assume it was ultimately a good thing, that I might not know why in the present, but when I succeeded in achieving my goal or navigating past it, I would eventually understand why.

I've also realised that obstacles will give me real-time feedback about the strength of passion I have concerning my ultimate goal. If I am just keenly interested, as opposed to truly passionate, some obstacles will stop me.

If I am truly passionate, nothing will stop me.

> "Nothing in this world is as powerful as an idea whose time has come."

Adversity makes us more resilient, thus, capable of withstanding challenges. The way you handle adversity defines you as a person.

Rising above particular circumstances is what allows you to live an extraordinary life.

Yet, as Michael Jordan alluded to in his quote above, failure is not something we can necessarily avoid; rather, it is part of the journey to success. It is important to learn to deal with challenges when they occur instead of feeling ashamed for not succeeding.

Furthermore, as Jordan relayed, when the time comes to take another shot, the most critical thing you can do is suit up, show up, and do your best, regardless of the events that took place the last time out.

As long as you continue to pursue your passions, you can never be a failure. Remember, failure is a temporary condition, we learn from shortfalls and mistakes and then continue on towards our goals.

I love this story. His schoolteacher told Thomas Alva Edison that he would never amount to anything. Later, he made countless attempts at creating a way to effectively use the power of electricity, capture sound, capture and project moving images, mine ore, and much more.

> *"I never quit until I get what I'm after. Negative results ... are just as valuable to me as positive results." Thomas Edison.*

Edison trained himself to derive positive energy from failures. This meant he would maintain positive, forward momentum whatever the outcome of his efforts.

Planning helps you tackle obstacles. The plan you made earlier will guide you to achieve your goals, especially if you take the time to plan for potential problems.

When planning for difficulties, do so in a structured way. What could that look like? See below for a simple, three-step process.

Step 1 – Identify likely obstacles (hurdles)

Step 2 – List the likely impacts if the obstacle appears or risk crystallises

Step 3 – Identify and record the mitigating actions you could take to avoid the issue or either successfully navigate it

Planning for problems gives you a variety of advantages:

- Helps you to foresee possible danger areas and plan accordingly, rather than just "reacting" at the time
- Allows you to channel your energy toward productive measures and confidence-building opportunities
- Allows your subconscious mind to rehearse responses well ahead of the need to act in reality; and
- Helps you stay afloat throughout the entire journey

Go back and look through your notebook. Read over your goals and blueprint for success. Think about any obstacles or difficulties and write them down in a special "Home Free" section. Then write possible solutions to every problem you've thought of.

I call this section "Home Free" because if you encounter one of the difficulties you've thought of—or even one that you haven't—you can look in the notebook for possible solutions, and you'll be Home Free!

When you encounter difficulties on your path, don't panic. South African statesman Nelson Mandela said,

> "The greatest glory of living lies not in never falling, but in rising every time you fall." Nelson Mandela

Continuously planning, adjusting plans, and evaluating what works, aligns with Michael Jordan's belief in persevering through tough times. Tweak your plans, rework your next move, and continue forward.

When you set up a situation where you strive for realistic but stretching goals and have a well-designed course, you have a chance of succeeding far beyond your wildest dreams.

In the words of the great American statesman Thomas Jefferson (1743 - 1826), who wrote the Declaration of Independence and served as the third U.S. President:

"Nothing can stop the man (or woman) with the right mental attitude from achieving his goal; nothing on earth can help the man (or woman) with the wrong mental attitude."

Choose your attitude. Choose your destination.

Dig deeper.....

1. **"The Dip: A Little Book That Teaches You When to Quit (and When to Stick)" by Seth Godin**
   - Seth Godin discusses "the dip," a challenging phase in any meaningful endeavour. He differentiates between a dip, which can lead to success, and a cul-de-sac or cliff, signalling when to quit. The book is a guide to understanding when to persevere and when strategic quitting is beneficial.

2. **"Man's Search for Meaning" by Viktor E. Frankl**
   - Viktor Frankl's memoir and philosophical work explore finding meaning through suffering. Introducing logotherapy, Frankl argues that purpose and meaning, not pleasure, are central to human life, especially when facing adversity.

3. **"The Obstacle Is the Way: The Timeless Art of Turning Trials into Triumph" by Ryan Holiday**
   - Ryan Holiday uses Stoicism and historical anecdotes to illustrate turning obstacles into opportunities. Focusing on perception, action, and will, Holiday offers a framework for overcoming challenges through internal strength.

4. **"Adversity Quotient: Turning Obstacles into Opportunities" by Paul G. Stoltz**
   - Paul Stoltz introduces the Adversity Quotient (AQ), a measure of dealing with adversity. He posits that AQ outweighs IQ and EQ in predicting success, providing strategies to enhance one's AQ for better problem-solving and performance.

5. **Research Paper: "The Benefits of Adversity" by R. Biswas-Diener**

    - This paper explores the positive outcomes of adversity, focusing on post-traumatic growth. It highlights how challenges can lead to personal growth, increased resilience, and a deeper appreciation of life.

CHAPTER 8.
TOASTING YOUR TRIUMPHS

"Celebrate what you want to see more of"
- Tom Peters

I love learning and always have done. As a kid, I had a relentless curiosity that has followed me into adulthood. For instance, when I was promoted into a challenging role early in my career, my commitment to personal development drove me to gain the skills required to succeed (delegation and change management), leading to a surprising but rewarding success.

This value of personal development was one of the first to emerge when I did the exercise to unearth my values. But I didn't call it personal development back then — just learning the skills I had seen in others and needed to be successful in my role.

I am driven and can easily see milestones achieved as nothing more than an activity to be ticked off, as I move to focus on the next thing.

I can remember working on a big project many years ago in the UK. There was a serious risk the project would fail, resulting in wasted costs and severe embarrassment for all involved. I didn't want to go there. Unfortunately, I became so obsessed with the outcomes that each time we made progress, I breathed a quiet sigh of relief and charged ahead.

Eventually, the team was worn down by this approach. They reported that their roles had become about avoiding problems instead of making a meaningful contribution to the plan. Research in neurology supports this; a study in the Journal of Positive Psychology found that positive reinforcement increases dopamine levels, enhancing motivation. This was evident when my team's morale and performance dipped due to a lack of recognition.

An urgent fix was required, so I considered a broad range of rewards. The rewards that worked were not huge or expensive and included allowing the team to leave slightly early, watch a sports event in the office, and start a little later. Small gifts like cinema tickets and restaurant vouchers always had a much greater impact than their equivalent in cash.

Likewise, your rewards to yourself don't have to be elaborate or expensive. It could be as simple as taking a break, going for a walk, or having that extra coffee. Doing this consistently will cause your brain to link positive emotions to progress, and it will automatically seek this kind of reward by doing more of the same – helping you achieve your goals.

While setting goals, remember to break them into manageable tasks. For example, if your goal is to improve in public speaking, start by speaking in small groups before progressing to larger audiences. Simultaneously, celebrate each step, like the first time you confidently finish a presentation without stumbling.

Alternatively, you might have a personal goal to, say, run a marathon. In training, you reach the point where you're able to run ten miles comfortably. That's cause for a celebration! Someone who has run countless marathons might not commend themselves for running ten miles; yet if you are not an experienced marathoner, ten miles, or even five, is a significant milestone in your training regime. It indicates you have stuck to the program and are committed to going the distance.

Picture this: You're in a job where every meaningful win gets a big thumbs up. Feels awesome, right? That's the kind of energy boost you give yourself every time you pat yourself on the back for your own wins!

Since you are the boss of goals and dreams, find ways to say thank you, pat yourself on the back, and express how proud you are of your accomplishments.

- **Recognise time and energy spent**—Acknowledge your productivity and the wise use of your time and energy.

- **Recognise the progress you've made**—When reaching for a goal, you have three options: advance, stagnate, or backslide. When you move forward and make progress, acknowledge that you are moving in the right direction. Each time you hit a target, celebrate. The larger the milestone, the greater the reward.

- **Recognise when you overcome a big hurdle**—This can be a great motivator to keep moving forward when things get tough. It also really allows you to log your progress.

Everyone, regardless of their background or profession, finds joy in celebrating accomplishments. It's a universal truth that resonates from the boardroom to the classroom. Not only does honouring a victory provide a sense of recognition of a job done well, but it also indicates that there is value to your efforts which motivates the recipient (you!) to achieve continued success.

During lull times, highlighting your accomplishments can provide the impetus to achieve the remaining component.

Take fund-raising campaigns, for example. They use big, bold markers on charts to show how much money has been raised. The higher the bar gets toward reaching the total goal, the more excited people become. This excitement then translates into increased contributions, which, in turn, fuels even more donations. You can create the same sort of excitement for yourself.

As a certified leadership and executive coach, having guided many through their self-improvement journeys, I've gained these insights not just from theory but from real-life successes and setbacks.

I have what I call my 'Small Wins Theory,' where I advocate for a series of incremental victories leading to major changes, an approach distinct from traditional goal-setting methods that often underestimate these small but significant triumphs.

According to L. Pakii Pierce, motivational speaker, and author, Think Well & Finish Strong, "The road to confidence is paved with weekly triumphs and victories."

Pierce believes that it is important to learn to applaud your achievements regularly as an act of faith and trust, indicating that you are neither ruled by fear nor self-doubt.

Pierce also explains that being grateful for what you already have accomplished can make you feel good about your energy output and, thus, more likely to continue working toward your goals.

Success is in the journey, not just the outcome.

Be sure to bask in the glory before the very end. You have earned each moment, and celebrating can help propel you further on your path.

> *"When you do the common things in life in an uncommon way, you will command the attention of the world."* —George Washington Carver (1864 - 1943), American horticulturist

Dig deeper...

1. **Think Well & Finish Strong, by L. Pakii Pierce.** Author and motivational speaker Pierce offers concrete, grounded information as to how you can overcome fear and other challenges to reach the goals you set for yourself. A big part of his message is appreciating all you have and have already accomplished. www.upgradeyourmind.com.

2. **Habits of Successful People: Hoops and Freedom, by Neel Raman.** In his e-book, author, keynote speaker, and coach Raman relays the importance of celebrating your victories to honour your struggles and share your triumphs with others. Hence, they feel comfortable doing the same. www.hoopsandfreedom.com.

3. **Winners Don't Quit...Today, They Call Me Doctor, by Pamela McCauley-Bell, Ph.D.** Focused on helping people "stay the course," Dr. McCauley-Bell's book and kit are intended to show how everyone experiences peaks and valleys and that the important thing is to hang in there and always try to do your best. McCauley-Bell's forte is enthusing young people about going into professions in engineering and technology.

4. **A Hand to Guide to Me, by Denzel Washington.** To honour the Boys and Girls Club of America's 100th anniversary, Washington crafted a collection of inspirational stories from more than 70 well-known personalities, including athletes, actors, and leadership figures. A moving and meaningful resource for anyone who is looking for a mentor, has acted as a mentor, or has worked with one. Each story has a celebratory component wherein they receive an unforgettable gift or engage in a memorable experience.

CHAPTER 9.
PERSEVERANCE PAYS: STAY THE COURSE

> *"Every great work, every great accomplishment, has been brought into manifestation through holding to the vision, and often just before the big achievement comes apparent failure and discouragement."*
> — **Florence Scovel Shinn (1871-1940)**
> **author of self-help books.**

By now, you'll know I was never strong in Math. I left school with no qualifications in this area but finally began to believe I would see progress here when I grasped Boolean Algebra (also known as Binary or Logical Algebra). I took this subject as part of a computer programming course which eventually progressed from entry-level to more advanced statistics.

Somehow, the application of statistical methods to real-life situations and processes just made sense and I quickly began to feature near the top of the class.

Then I started a foundation course in accountancy in October 1986, and one year later, my math world completely unraveled again. You see, I had to take a compulsory subject called Quantitative Analysis, and a combination of short timelines, questionable application on my part, and low confidence resulted in failure.

This was called a 'gateway' subject, which you had to pass to proceed to the next stage, as competency in this area was fundamental to your chances of success in the programme.

I remember the potent mixture of hopelessness, fear, and embarrassment when I got my result. I knew it was marginal but had hoped I would somehow scrape through. It wasn't to be.

Failing this paper was particularly disappointing because I was doing so well in all other subjects, slightly surprising myself as I had not previously studied alongside such academically accomplished people.

As this was a gateway paper, I was told there might be a chance to retake the paper if your original mark suggested - with additional work and support - you might make the grade. Huge relief followed when I learned I was in this category, but I had genuinely given it my best shot (my view has changed in retrospect!), and I didn't know where to go.

This is where I learned one of my most powerful lessons in humility. I suddenly realised that I had to acknowledge the gap and do whatever it took to get the right help; I sought out the most competent mathematician in the group and told him my story, including my lack of math qualifications (his first question was – how did you get in?! A long story for another time) and how I would do anything for him to coach me up to the required standard.

After his initial shock, he graciously agreed to help me but insisted, I go back to school-level math and learn some of the foundational stuff I was missing. Not only was this an embarrassing gap to address, but it was also on top of revising the old content.

In later life I have become familiar with the saying that you "slow down to speed up". Sometimes the only way to move forward is to take a quick step back. It is what the military might call a "tactical withdrawal" as opposed to surrender but I wasn't giving up on my objective. I had long since decided that was not an option.

I would approach it differently because I wanted a vastly different outcome.

Long story short, my great friend Rupert Bruce tutored me to success, and we formed a friendship that continues today, although contact is all too infrequent.

I learned the hard way when you hit a brick wall, some of the core ingredients for continuing are:

1. Decide you're not giving up. Even if you feel you're done. Don't allow your emotions to determine your destiny.
2. Be curious about alternative routes and novel options.
3. Be humble.
4. Seek help – then accept it even if the terms are less than ideal. Remember, we are talking about short-term inconvenience for long-term benefits.
5. Only listen to those who are positive about what's possible and support your goals/ dreams.
6. As the saying goes, "keep your eyes on the prize" and go to work. It will get you there....

Next, I want to talk about "the wall" but using a different example to the one used earlier. Remember this is the point where you honestly believe you can't go one step further. You might feel as if you're swimming upstream or the passion that was once overflowing has nearly evaporated.

Whatever the reason, so long as you sincerely believe your goal is worth attaining, never give up. Quitting may look easier, but it is never satisfying. After all, your dreams are still out there to be lived into.

And if you don't fulfil your purpose, no one else can because it is unique to you.

Have you heard about the gold miner who quit only a few feet from hitting a huge gold vein? H. Ross Perot business magnate and US presidential candidate said,

> "Most people give up just when they're about to achieve success. They quit on the one-yard line. They give up at the last minute of the game, one foot from a winning touchdown."

Your plan may require a complete re-think; it may be more achievable by breaking the remaining steps into smaller, more manageable parts. If you're overwhelmed by the sheer enormity of having to do the daily footwork, choose to believe that, eventually, all will fall into place.

You may need a few days off to rejuvenate and get a fresh perspective. That's ok, as long as you don't stray too long or too far.

When you need a pick-me-up:

1. Ask advice from those who have achieved what you are looking to accomplish.
2. If you can't speak with them directly, read books they have written, watch videos they have shared, or read blogs they have posted.
3. Ask for assistance from others who can do the things you find difficult.

Even the most cursory of investigations will show you that every successful person has engaged the assistance of others. Edison built a laboratory with thousands of people working for him to help with his inventions. Athletes and entrepreneurs have coaches. Business owners bring in talent who can do things that the owners aren't good at or don't like to do.

Jack Welch, the famous CEO of General Electric (GE) made it a practice to hire people he considered more capable than himself. His rationale was clear - choose people more talented and you achieve better results. Some may not have said this of Jack Welch, but there is a degree of humility shown here.

Two American psychologists, David Dunning & Jason Kruger won a noble prize in 2000 for what they called the *Dunning-Kruger Effect*. We might call it *The Smartest Person In The Room Syndrome*. It is essentially the opposite of the more widely understood *Imposter Syndrome*.

> *"If you are the smartest person in the room, you're probably in the wrong room"* Rich Litvin - International Coach

The risks of the Dunning-Kruger effect are almost opposite to those of someone with imposter syndrome where they believe they are not good enough, were lucky, in the right place at the right time etc. Dunning Kruger makes you less likely to listen and learn, which results from a lack of awareness and can lead to disastrous risks due to overestimated confidence.

Yes, it's your dream and you will have the final say on how to move forward, but take all the counsel you can get from trusted contacts, then distil this down to your next best steps.

A small aside.

It has been said that ants are far better goal achievers than humans—they never give up. Just take a look at the power of these tiny insects. They:

- Follow instructions;
- Are determined;
- See defeat as temporary as opposed to permanent (absolutely critical distinction);
- Collaborate better with their peers (or colleagues);
- Defend what they have and expand upon it;
- Don't let personalities get in the way;
- Save their resources for future use;
- Expect more for themselves than they should (as exhibited by the fact they carry items 20 times their size); and
- Remain focused until they succeed (never give up).

Be ant-like in your commitment to the outcome you truly desire.

Remember the quote right at the start of this book:

"The moment one definitely commits oneself, then providence moves too…Whatever you can do or dream, you can - begin it. Boldness has genius, power, and magic in it. Begin it now."
– Goethe

When you make a definite move, providence will move. There will be synchronicities, things will naturally align. It will not necessarily make things easy, but you will be given support and encouragement along the way – often the type you would never have expected.

Try it and see. I can't explain it, but I think you'll be amazed by who you meet, what you see, what you hear, and how the world seems to align with your plan.

World-famous clothing designer Ralph Lauren said, "A leader has the vision and conviction that a dream can be achieved. He/she inspires the power and energy to get it done."

Who is to say what is a realistic goal? Who cares if it is what you truly desire? Anything is possible when you put your mind to it.

Sometimes reaching your goal may take longer than you thought. No problem, revise your plan. There may be more steps to take than you originally considered. Again, no problem. Just change your plan.

Along the way, you might discover that your goal is different from what you wanted in the first place. For instance, you may need help finding a connection between your chosen goal and your values or purpose.

That's ok, too. You have learned a valuable lesson about yourself, your expectations, and your desires to transform your life.

Sometimes it is only through trial and error and a process of elimination that we learn what we do want. If that is the case, go back to the beginning, discover your true passions, create a new plan, and go for it!

By allowing yourself the opportunity to gain perspective, you can see the cause of the problem. You may have been pushing too hard and could benefit from a more relaxed pace, or you may need to rev up the activity to experience some of the positive effects. Whatever the reason, these adjustments are a natural part of the journey toward your success, so don't allow yourself to become despondent.

Most importantly, don't belittle or shame yourself because you are struggling. Become familiar with the following framework and develop your mental toughness because:

> "Mental toughness is persistence, not intensity"
> **James Clear.**

The 4 C's model of Mental Toughness

The 4 C's Model of Mental is a framework formed of four key components: *Control, Commitment, Challenge,* and *Confidence*. Each of these components contributes to an individual's ability to demonstrate mental toughness in various situations, whether in sports, education, or professional environments.

1. **Control**: This aspect refers to the ability to manage your emotions and maintain self-discipline in challenging situations. It involves having a sense of influence over one's life events and reactions, highlighting the importance of emotional regulation and internal control.

2. **Commitment**: This element is about setting goals and being persistent in achieving them. It implies a tendency to be proactive and involved, rather than passive. Commitment in the context of mental toughness means being reliable and focused on tasks or objectives, demonstrating resilience in the face of obstacles (hurdles).

3. **Challenge**: Individuals with mental toughness see challenges as opportunities rather than threats. This component emphasises adaptability and the willingness to embrace change. It involves seeing challenges as a chance for growth and development, rather than as insurmountable problems.

4. **Confidence**: This relates to having a strong belief in your abilities and maintaining a positive attitude even in adversity. Confidence in the 4 C's model is not just about being sure of your skills, but also includes an element of belief in your ability to influence others and impose yourself on situations, when necessary.

The 4 C's model suggests that mental toughness is multidimensional, involving both emotional and cognitive aspects. It underscores the idea that mental toughness can be developed and enhanced through targeted strategies and practices.

So if you think you're not born this way, maybe you're right but you <u>choose it</u> by practising the disciplines listed above.

Michael Laskow of <u>www.taxi.com</u> offers this familiar advice:

"Don't quit when the going gets tough. People frequently quit when they're only inches from the finish line. The problem is, they don't know that one more inch, one more day, or for that matter, one more song, may be all that's necessary to achieve your dreams."

Dig deeper....

1. **"Developing Mental Toughness: Coaching Strategies to Improve Performance, Resilience and Wellbeing" by Doug Strycharczyk and Peter Clough**: This book provides a comprehensive guide to developing mental toughness. It covers coaching strategies that help enhance performance, resilience, and wellbeing, making it a valuable resource for coaches and trainers.

2. **"The Inner Game of Work" by Timothy Gallwey**: Gallwey explores the concept of the 'inner game' in the workplace context. The book focuses on overcoming mental barriers and maximizing potential, offering insights into achieving professional success through internal mental practices.

3. **"Grit: The Power of Passion and Perseverance" by Angela Duckworth**: Duckworth's book delves into the role of grit—defined as passion and perseverance for long-term goals—in achieving success. It combines personal anecdotes with research to demonstrate how perseverance and passion outweigh talent alone.

4. **Research - "Factorial validity of the mental toughness questionnaire-48" by Perry, Clough, Crust, and Earle**: This study validates a questionnaire designed to measure mental toughness based on the 4 C's model, providing a reliable tool for assessing this trait.

5. **Research - "Identifying the cognitive basis of mental toughness" by Dewhurst et al. (2012)**: This research investigates the cognitive aspects of mental toughness. The study suggests that mentally tough individuals experience less interference from unwanted memories, indicating a cognitive basis for mental toughness.

CHAPTER 10.
BELIEVE IN YOURSELF AND WATCH MAGIC HAPPEN

"Everything you need you already have. You are complete right now; you are a whole, total person, not an apprentice person on the way to someplace else. Your completeness must be understood by you and experienced in your thoughts as your own personal reality."
— **Wayne Dyer, motivational speaker**

Yes! You are magnificent! Inside you are all the keys to your success. It is only a matter of unlocking the doors and walking through. You have the will, skill and ability to gain the knowledge and experience you need to achieve your dreams: the drive and the passion is within you.

When you follow the suggestions in this book, you will have created your own, personal blueprint for success. While going through some of these steps, you will probably question what you truly want out of life, reassess your priorities and clarify your values. You will be on a path of learning new skills, beliefs, and habits that will increase your self-empowerment and happiness.

Well-known author Alice Walker says, "Don't wait around for other people to be happy for you. Any happiness you get, you've got to make yourself." It is empowering and freeing when you understand that you, alone, decide what dreams, goals, and actions will create a sense of personal fulfilment and hope in your life on a consistent basis; that every day, when you open your eyes, it is up to you to decide whether you will be happy or miserable, whether you are going to take actions toward your goals or away from them.

Always feed yourself the good stuff of life: meaningful relationships, pleasurable pastimes, enriching experiences, and purposeful interactions with others.

We'll finish with this. Highly skilled as a negotiator, military veteran, manager and leader, Colin Powell remains subject of much fascination. Listening to his audiences, peers, and rookies, Powell is known to be a proponent of not watching the clock and not shutting any doors.

General Colin Powell's Rules for life:

1. It isn't as bad as you think. It will look better in the morning.
2. Get mad; then get over it.
3. Avoid having your ego so close to your position that when your position falls, your ego goes with it.
4. It can be done!
5. Be careful what you choose. You may get it.
6. Don't let adverse facts stand in the way of a good decision.
7. You can't make someone else's choices. You shouldn't let someone else make yours.
8. Check small things.
9. Share credit.
10. Remain calm. Be kind.
11. Have a vision. Be demanding.
12. Don't take counsel of your fears or naysayers.
13. Perpetual optimism is a force multiplier.

Closing statement

"Success is ninety-nine percent mental attitude. It calls for love, joy, optimism, confidence, serenity, poise, faith, courage, cheerfulness, imagination, initiative, tolerance, honesty, humility, patience, and enthusiasm. . . . Success is having the courage to meet failure without being defeated. It is refusing to let present loss interfere with your long-range goal. . . . Success is relative and individual and personal. It is your answer to the problem of making your minutes, hours, days, weeks, months, and years add up to a great life."
—Wilfred A. Peterson, Author

APPENDIX 1

Purpose Clarification Exercise

Guidance

It is worth noting people with high levels of **eudemonic** well-being —which involves having a sense of purpose along with a sense of control and a feeling like what you do is worthwhile — tend to live longer. Other researchers found that well-being might be protective for health maintenance.

Research also links feeling as if you have a sense of purpose to positive health outcomes such as fewer strokes and heart attacks, better sleep, and a lower risk of dementia and disabilities.

A 2016 study published in the *Journal of Research and Personality* found that individuals who feel a sense of purpose make more money than those who think their work lacks meaning.

Now that's good news! You do not have to choose between having wealth and living a meaningful life. You might find the more purpose you have, the more money you'll earn, if that's a motivator.

With all those benefits, finding purpose and meaning in your life is important. But purpose and meaning are something that takes time to determine.

The process requires plenty of self-reflection, listening to others, and finding where your passions lie.

Approach

1. Answer the questions below. Answer them all.

APPENDIX 1

2. Once all the questions have been answered, go back through them, and look for recurring themes or roles in your answers.

3. Note these themes/ roles on a separate sheet of paper or another page. Then take a break – a proper break measured in hours, at least 24.

   - I suggest this because it gives your subconscious mind time to do its work and add to the great work you have started.

4. Test what you find with people you know and trust. If some will try to talk you into doing what is predictable, expected/ acceptable, DO NOT engage them in this process.

5. Looking at your answers below, what do they suggest you should do with your life?

In answering this question, you must focus on the ideal or the perfect. It does not mean you will get there, nor do you need to, but coming up with a purpose that is not based on the reasonable, acceptable, or expected is fundamentally important to the exercise.

Let your heart take you wherever it goes.

Trust yourself. The answer is within you because you were designed with it in mind.

Sam's Purpose

> *"To release potential in people that positively impacts the world today and future generations."*

I am obsessed with continuing education and releasing potential. It drives my family crazy – in a good way 😊

I also hate inequality while loving competition. It took me some time to get there. Still, it makes my life's work of designing and delivering customised leadership development programs for senior executives - in the competitive business world - absolutely perfect for me.

I have further enhanced my Purpose by taking on a much bigger challenge – one I have no idea how to implement, but I am committed to it, nonetheless.

I aim to revolutionise English-speaking Africa by releasing potential in communities and individuals through pro bono coaching services.

I took this approach because it honours the people of Africa; we know that talent and desire exist. There is a growing belief amongst the people. I want to help by providing some tools for the revolution.

Questions

- What desires have been living in me most of my life?

  ....
  ....
  ....
  ....

- What motivates me to work hard and be productive?

  ....
  ....
  ....
  ....

- How do I want to be remembered? What do I want my legacy to be?

  ....
  ....
  ....
  ....

- What keeps me going forward when I am worn out?

  ....
  ....
  ....
  ....

APPENDIX 1

- What makes me refuse to quit when I meet with resistance?

  ....
  ....
  ....
  ....

- What do I do that does not seem like work?

  ....
  ....
  ....
  ....

- What do I do that brings a positive response and support from people?

  ....
  ....
  ....
  ....

- What am I doing or what is happening in my life when doors seem to open automatically and effortlessly?

  ....
  ....
  ....
  ....

- What do wise leaders/counselors think about my work?

  ....
  ....
  ....
  ....

- What makes me feel good about being who I am?

  ....
  ....
  ....
  ....

- What makes my creative juices flow?

  ....
  ....
  ....
  ....

- What did I do as a kid that I no longer do and miss?

  ....
  ....
  ....
  ....

- What injustices really bother me?

  ....
  ....
  ....
  ....

- What problem is bigger than me that I would love to help fix or make a difference to?

  ....
  ....
  ....
  ....

- What am I willing to sacrifice to accomplish it?

  ....
  ....
  ....
  ....

- What would I do without being paid for it if I could afford to?

  ....
  ....
  ....
  ....

For those in a faith-based communities:

- What am I doing that I would be proud to offer for God's approval?

  ....
  ....
  ....
  ....

- What would I be willing to withstand Satan/ evil forces to accomplish?

  ....
  ....
  ....
  ....

Enjoy the process.

Produced and modified with the permission of the International Coaching Federation (ICF)

APPENDIX 2

Values clarification exercise

Guidance

This is going to be a great exercise. Please bear in mind that there are no right or wrong answers.

Other points to note:

- You do not have to do this on your own. Feel free to ask others for input.
    - Questions like 'How would you describe me?' or 'What would you say my strengths are?' can help fill out the picture – but they are not the answer!
- You will uncover your Values – they are already there. So, if they are not showing up, be patient with yourself because they will.
- Take your time. Do this work when you are feeling relaxed.
    - You do not have to do it in a hit (in fact, I'd encourage you not to). And you can come up with a list that you revisit and, ultimately, change as your awareness grows.
- Sometimes being clear about what you have a deep dislike or distrust for reveals your values. So, while you will generally focus on what you want/ admire/ like through this exercise, occasionally, the opposite of what you want or admire can be a powerful indicator of a deeply held value.

Approach

1. Answer the questions below. Answer them all.
2. Once all the questions are answered, go back through them and look for recurring themes or words in your answers.
3. Note these themes/ words on a separate sheet of paper or another page. Then take a break – a proper break measured in hours, at least 24.
   - I always suggest this because it gives your subconscious mind time to do its work and add to the great work you have started.
4. See if any of the themes/words overlap. For instance, honesty might coincide with integrity, so you may choose the one that best captures the value you want to recognise.
5. List this new set of themes/ words after you've completed point 4.
6. Choose the top 5 (six at a stretch) of your Values, represented by the list of themes/words. Ideally, you will choose a single word that captures each value, e.g., trust, transparency, reliability, etc.
   - If you come up with as few as three values, no problem. Fewer would be OK, too; I have just never seen it.

Sam's Values (I use an acronym – S.O.A.P.P.I).

I have listed my core values below to make this more real and less daunting. You will note that I don't follow my guidance because my first value is a statement, not a single word - *Service to others*!!

The point here is this is all guidance, not rules. Do your thing to get to the answer that best reflects you.

My Values are:

1. **S**ervice to others
2. **O**ptimism
3. **A**ccountability
4. **P**ersonal development (I could have chosen *Growth*, for instance)

5. **P**erseverance (could easily have been *Tenancity*)
6. **I**ntegrity

Obviously, I made the acronym up after I had identified my Values. Still, I regularly check in and ask myself, especially when I'm not feeling right, "Am I living *SOAPPI?*" Because if I don't live my values, I automatically feel off.

Make sense?

Questions

- Describe a time when life was good. What made life good, then?

  ....
  ....
  ....
  ....

- When have you felt really powerful? Why?

  ....
  ....
  ....
  ....

- What are you most pleased and proud of having accomplished? (list at least three things).

  ....
  ....
  ....
  ....

APPENDIX 2

- When in your life are you most at peace and content with yourself?

  ....
  ....
  ....
  ....

- What are your strengths?

  ....
  ....
  ....
  ....

- What would you do with your life if you knew you wouldn't fail and were certain of financial prosperity?

  ....
  ....
  ....
  ....

- Which people in your life do you trust the most? Why?

  ....
  ....
  ....
  ....

- Who do you admire? Why?

  ....
  ....
  ....
  ....

- Who do you dislike/ find it impossible to connect with? Why?

  ....
  ....
  ....
  ....

- How would you want people to describe you?

  ....
  ....
  ....
  ....

- How do you want to be treated/wish to treat others?

  ....
  ....
  ....
  ....

- What does it mean to be a good community member or a good citizen?

  ....
  ....
  ....
  ....

- What does it mean to be a good parent/ partner?

  ....
  ....
  ....
  ....

APPENDIX 2

- What does it mean to be a good friend?

  ....
  ....
  ....
  ....

- What does it mean to be a good colleague?

  ....
  ....
  ....
  ....

- Where would you like to make a difference in the world?

  ....
  ....
  ....
  ....

- What legacy will you leave? How do you want to be remembered?

  ....
  ....
  ....
  ....

Enjoy the process.

Produced and modified with the permission of the International Coaching Federation (ICF)

APPENDIX 3

Stephen Covey's Prioritisation and Time Management tool

- Add tasks in box 1 for what is urgent and important - manage these tasks, the best you can.

- Spend most of your time in box 2. Focus here on things that deliver long-term benefits.

- Do all you can to avoid activities that fall into box/quadrants 3 and 4.

	URGENT	**NON URGENT**
IMPORTANT		
NOT IMPORTANT		

SEED BUSINESS ASSOCIATES

www.ingramcontent.com/pod-product-compliance
Lightning Source LLC
Chambersburg PA
CBHW072014290426
44109CB00018B/2238